Shall Roger Casement Hang?

by

Peter Arnott

Vagabond Voices
Glasgow

© Peter Arnott 2016

First published in April 2016 by
Vagabond Voices Publishing Ltd.,
Glasgow,
Scotland.

ISBN 978-1-908251-66-4

The author's right to be identified as author of this book under the Copyright, Designs and Patents Act 1988 has been asserted.

Printed and bound in Poland

Cover design by Mark Mechan

Typeset by Park Productions

The publisher acknowledges subsidy towards this publication from Creative Scotland

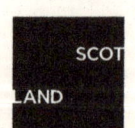

ALBA | CHRUTHACHAIL

For further information on Vagabond Voices, see the website,
www.vagabondvoices.co.uk

Introduction

At the time of going to press, this play has been written and workshopped but not yet performed. It is due to open on May 20th 2016 with Benny Young as Casement and Stevie Clyde as Hall – and everybody else – at the Tron Theatre in Glasgow directed by Andy Arnold.

Sometimes, it's all about the present tense. This is particularly true when working on a story that is almost exactly a hundred years old and a play that is being published before the first performance. Firstly the play is about the Irish Independence struggle at a time when Ireland is very largely reimagining itself, especially with regard to homosexuality. On the fiftieth anniversary of the Easter Rising (when Casement was disinterred from Pentonville Gaol and reburied – against his wishes – in Glasnevin Cemetery in Dublin), it was still conventional wisdom in Irish Republican circles that the British had forged the notorious "Black Diaries" that recounted the sex life of this most complex and the contradictory of complex and contradictory revolutionaries of 1916. In Ireland itself the centenary is being marked with nuances and negotiations that owe as much to what happened in the years after the celebrations of 1966, which fed into the Civil Rights struggle in the North, as they do to the ways in which Irish Society is reimagining itself on both sides of the 1921 border.

Secondly, in a Scotland where, had the referendum gone the other way, we would be in the early weeks of independence ourselves, the "present-tenseness" of events around the Easter Rising suggests a play about the beginning of what Tom Nairn called "The Break Up of Britain".

Thirdly and most importantly for the way the play is written, there is a general problem with historical drama, and that is in deciding what the present tense of the play is, particularly in a context where a good many of the first audience (this being Glasgow) will know a good deal of that history, but rather more of the audience (it not being Ireland) will know little or nothing.

I had thought initially that the present would be Casement in between his sentence of death (on June 28th 1916) and his execution (on August 3rd of that year), and that we and he would look back on his long and varied career as a British Diplomat, Irish revolutionary and human rights pioneer, while the prototypical Special Branch was surreptitiously destroying his reputation by circulating the "Black Diaries". But when I looked at the partial transcripts of Casement's two days of interrogation at Scotland Yard immediately after his capture, which took place on Easter Sunday and Easter Monday, I quickly saw that, in the contrasting circumstances of those two days, both Casement and the British thought on the Sunday that the Rising had been called off, and both were shocked when it actually happened at noon on Easter Monday. Here was a 'present tense' when what everyone knows happened hasn't happened yet."

It then became my job to shoehorn all the complexity and ambiguity I've felt about Casement into those two days ... as well as the memories and prophecies, the past and future tenses evoked in that present. The help of Andy and the actors in doing that was invaluable as was the support of the Playwrights' Studio, Scotland.

I hope that on the stage and page what follows will intrigue and provoke both the historically informed and the committed, this being about Ireland, God help me as a Scotsman! It's too late to change it now.

That's the problem with the present tense. It's over before you know it.

Peter Arnott, Glasgow, 30 March 2016

Shall Roger Casement Hang?

DRAMATIS PERSONAE

SIR ROGER CASEMENT, 53, a former civil servant from Antrim,

REGINALD HALL, 40, an intelligence Officer in the Royal Navy from Scotland

A constable in the Royal Irish Constabulary from Ulster

A priest of Tralee, Co. Kerry

A Welsh soldier

and recorded voices representing

GEORGE BERNARD SHAW, an Irish playwright

ELIMA, a twelve year old from the Congo

The action is continuous. The "present tense" of this play about events one hundred years ago is the two days of interrogation undergone by Roger Casement in Scotland Yard on 23 and 24 April 1916. Other events from the "past and future tenses" are portrayed by means of different, less "realistic/psychological" theatrical conventions based on contemporary documents. The whole play takes place in the shadow of the scaffold that awaits Casement.

SCENE 1

George Bernard Shaw, *Manchester Guardian*, 2 August 1916

As we open, CASEMENT waits on stage. The gibbet is tested with a sandbag. CASEMENT watches as the trapdoor opens and the bag is dropped to test the mechanism. As the scaffold is tested, we hear the valediction of GEORGE BERNARD SHAW on an old recording.

SHAW: George Bernard Shaw, Manchester Guardian, August the second 1916.

"Shall Roger Casement hang?" In Ireland, Roger Casement will be regarded as a national hero if he is executed, and quite possibly as a British spy if he is not. For that reason it may well be that he would object very strongly to my attempt here today to prevent his canonisation. But Ireland has had enough heroes and martyrs already, and if England has not by this time had enough of manufacturing those martyrs in fits of ill temper, then experience is thrown away on her.

SCENE 2

Scotland Yard, London: Easter Sunday, 23 April 1916

CASEMENT waits for interrogation in a room with a table and a sink. The second actor enters. He is urbane, confident, educated, Scottish. Takes his time.

HALL: (*removing CASEMENT's handcuffs*) No need for those. Sit down.

CASEMENT: (*sitting, wary of HALL's politeness, but instinctively grateful for it*) Thank you.

HALL: How was your journey? You look a bit tired I must say!

CASEMENT: Yes. I am tired.

HALL: Not so easy to sleep? Was it not? Have you eaten?

CASEMENT: They gave me breakfast in Liverpool. At the station. Everyone's been very kind.

HALL: Good. That's good. (*HALL sits, pause*) I suppose I should ask you now officially. What is your name?

CASEMENT: (*smiles wearily*) You know my name, I think. I should ask you for yours.

HALL: I'm so sorry. Hall ... Captain Reginald Hall. Royal Navy. You were found on the coast, do you see? That brought you into my bailiwick, as it were. So... What is your name?

CASEMENT is silent.

HALL: Oh really! Are we going to play that game? (*sighs, pause*) On your arrest on Friday, you said to the Royal Irish Constabulary that your name was "Richard Morten". Why did you do that? (*pause*) You had one visitor in the police station in Tralee. The parish priest. Did you tell him your real name? What else did you tell him? (*pause*) Who is Richard Morten?

CASEMENT: (*answering easily*) Richard is an old friend of mine. His was the first name that came into my head.

He smiles. HALL looks at him for a moment, thinking about CASEMENT's decision to speak.

HALL: A friend of yours? Is he a dear friend of yours?

CASEMENT: (*one sentence leading him to the next*) Richard is my dearest friend in England. I think he's my dearest friend anywhere. It may be that I did him no great favour by taking his name ... or by naming him as my friend just now. I was thinking of him the moment before I saw the policeman. It was all entirely coincidental.

HALL: His name just came to you?

CASEMENT: Yes.

HALL: For no particular reason? You don't have any papers ... in that name?

CASEMENT: No.

HALL: In fact, you had no identification of any kind, did you?

CASEMENT: No.

HALL: So why him?

CASEMENT: Well, he's English, of course. I suppose ... I thought...

HALL: (*jocular*) Aha! You thought you should disguise yourself as an Englishman?

He laughs. Pause. HALL's technique is to wait, knowing now that CASEMENT will be unable to resist filling a silence.

CASEMENT: (*a shared confidence that he expects to be understood*) Well ... it's hardly the first time.

HALL: (*smiling*) What does that mean?

CASEMENT: In my career. That I have... You know... Over the years, I have developed a variety of voices. I was working for the British Colonial Service. You're in the navy. You must understand.

HALL: No. Understand what?

CASEMENT: You're Scottish. Aren't you?

HALL: I don't follow.

CASEMENT: It must have been your experience, as it has been my experience...

HALL: (*interrupting*) No.

CASEMENT: Really?

HALL: No.

Pause. CASEMENT laughs nervously. HALL takes him in for a moment then changes tack.

HALL: Richard Morten. Of Denham in Buckinghamshire. You didn't make that up, then? He's real?

CASEMENT: (*still trying to be light*) Oh, yes. And he's entirely unconnected to any of this business. I imagine he'll be horrified at the whole thing. I shall have to apologise to him the first chance I get... (*HALL writes*) I assure you he's quite innocent. I assure you.

HALL smiles. Keeps writing. Stops. Waits, smiling encouragingly. CASEMENT decides to try something else he's had in mind.

CASEMENT: May I see someone? I'd like to see someone. It could be in your presence. It would be someone you would approve of.

HALL: "Someone I would approve of?" Who's that?

CASEMENT: Sir William Tyrrell.

HALL writes.

HALL: Sir William Tyrrell?

CASEMENT: Yes.

HALL: The senior civil servant.

CASEMENT: Yes.

HALL: A much more senior civil servant than I am?

CASEMENT: If you want to put it that way ... yes.

HALL: Are you trying to intimidate me?

CASEMENT: No. Of course not. He's a friend.

HALL: Are you trying to make me afraid of you?

CASEMENT: No ... it's very simple... I should like to see a friendly face... I haven't seen one since I...

HALL: Are you trying to make an impression on me with your eminent connections?

CASEMENT: No... I should simply like to see him.

HALL: But why would you like to see him? What for?

CASEMENT: I've told you...

HALL: What help d'you think Sir William could be to you ... in your position?

Pause.

CASEMENT: May I see him?

HALL: It's Easter Sunday. I doubt very much he's in town. (*considers, then*) If I were to get word to Sir William of your ... request ... how does that help me? Put it that way.

CASEMENT: He can testify to my character.

HALL: (*a startled laugh, then*) This isn't an interview for a job, you know! I'm not taking up your references. You do understand that?

CASEMENT: (*with his first hint of irritation*) Of course I understand that.

HALL: Do you? Do you really appreciate what your position is? Do you really understand what it is you've done?

Pause.

CASEMENT: I think so.

Pause.

HALL: Sir William has just been named as His Majesty's Ambassador in Paris.

CASEMENT: Oh. I'm delighted to hear that. He's a very good man.

HALL: Yes. He's a very good man. So forgive me... Why on earth would a "very good man" like Sir

William Tyrrell want to give you a character reference? I'm not to suspect Sir William Tyrrell of being in sympathy with treason, am I?

CASEMENT: Of course not ... but he may be in sympathy with me. (*HALL looks at him disbelievingly, then*) May I see him?

HALL: Richard Morten ... of Denham ... in Buckinghamshire. Should I be seeing him?

CASEMENT: (*alarmed*) Now, I've told you, you're not to think anything of my naming him. I named him by pure chance.

HALL: As you have named Sir William Tyrrell ... the most prominent Irishman serving in the Foreign Office ... by pure chance?

CASEMENT: Richard and I campaigned together ... on the Congo campaign ... the anti-slavery campaign ... years ago. Sir William and I ... were colleagues... (*HALL writes, allowing CASEMENT to ramble on in his self-incriminating way*) Please... There's nothing sinister in a man having friends... (*HALL looks at him, he tries to be firm*) Now, look... Neither Richard nor Sir William nor anyone else...

HALL looks up at him with a face of stone. CASEMENT tails off in the face of HALL's scorn.

HALL: Yes? "Neither Richard nor Sir William or anyone else"...what?

CASEMENT: (*eventually*) You're right. I'm sorry. I was wrong to mention them. They are friends of mine ... from a past life. That life ... is over. Our old fellowship is a casualty of war. I should forget my friends. I should reflect that I don't have friends any more... I forgot myself. Would you do me the great favour ... Captain Hall ... of forgetting my weakness? I should not have named my friends.

HALL: (*looks up, smiles sadly, forgivingly*) This is England. An innocent man has nothing to fear. But you must be more careful of what you say.

He tears up the papers he's been writing on, to CASEMENT's *relief.*

SCENE 3

Banna Strand Beach, County Kerry: Two days earlier, Good Friday, 21 April 1916

The sound of lapping waves. CASEMENT *sits looking out to sea.*

CASEMENT'S VOICE (VO): Swamped and swimming ashore on an unknown strand, I was happy for the first time in more than a year. Although I knew what fate awaited me, I cannot tell you what I felt. The sandhills were full of skylarks rising in the dawn – the first sound I heard through the surf was their song as I waded through the breakers and they kept rising all the time to the old rath at Currashone. And all around were primroses and wild violets and the singing of skylarks in the air and I was back in Ireland again.

CASEMENT crumples paper in his hand and lies prostrate on the sand. After some moments, a CONSTABLE of the RIC approaches him, pointing a gun.

CONSTABLE: (*Northern Irish*) Get up. Get yer hauns oan yer heyud.

CASEMENT: If I put my hands on my head, I can't get up. Sorry.

CONSTABLE: Get up first ... THEN put yer hauns on yer head.

CASEMENT does. He drops the piece of paper. The CONSTABLE doesn't seem to notice. The CONSTABLE kicks CASEMENT's bag.

CONSTABLE: Open it... (*CASEMENT hesitates*) Open it!

CASEMENT: Am I to get back down again?

CONSTABLE: Open the fucking thing!

CASEMENT opens the bag. The CONSTABLE glances at it. CASEMENT reaches a hand into the bag.

CONSTABLE: Get out of that ... get the fuck out of that!

The CONSTABLE is now stuck. He can't open the bag himself without dropping his guard on CASEMENT.

CASEMENT: Be calm. Please.

CONSTABLE: Shut up.

CASEMENT: You don't need to worry about me. (*tries to be jocular*) This seems a very peculiar way to greet an English tourist. (*laughs, pause, tries to find out where he is*) Where are you stationed...?

CONSTABLE: Yer all wet, look at ye.

CASEMENT: I fell. On the strand. My name is Richard Morten.

CONSTABLE: Did I ask you what your fucking name is? (*pause*) Where you stayin'? The hotel?

CASEMENT: I've only just arrived... I haven't...

CONSTABLE: Did ye fall off a fucking boat? Look at ye!

CASEMENT: From Dublin ... this morning...

CONSTABLE: On the train? Show's yer ticket!

CASEMENT: (*tries to be light*) I really don't think you have any right...

CONSTABLE: I do. I fucking do. Defence of the Fuckin Realm... I can ask you any fucking thing I feel like. Keep your fucking hands where I can see them. What's your address?

CASEMENT: The Savoy, Denham ... Buckinghamshire.

CONSTABLE: What the fuck are you doin in the shit-stained back end of fucking nowhere? Exactly?

CASEMENT: (*pause*) You're not from round here, are you?

CONSTABLE: What?

CASEMENT: You're from the North ... aren't you... You're stationed out west to keep an eye on the natives?

CONSTABLE: How dae you know that? Mister Savoy Denham fucking Buckinghamshire?

CASEMENT: I've been to Ireland many times.

CONSTABLE: Oh aye?

CASEMENT: I'm writing a book about St Brendan ... he was from around here...

CONSTABLE: The saints drip off the fuckin walls round here...

CASEMENT: Yes.

CONSTABLE: Ignorant, superstitious, priest-ridden, treacherous fucking savages.

CASEMENT: I have family ... I have many friends ... in County Antrim... (*the CONSTABLE looks at him*). As I say, I arrived in Dublin last night. I took the train... Where are your people from? Where do you...

CONSTABLE: Yer papers in your bag, are they?

CASEMENT: What papers?

CONSTABLE: What papers? There's a fucking war on...

CASEMENT: Well...

CONSTABLE: Show me your papers!

CASEMENT: (*a hint of irritation*) How can I do that with my hands on my head? How am I to reach into my bag or into my pockets if you want me to keep my hands where you can see them?

CONSTABLE: Right. Tell you what, old fruit... I'm going to kneel down and put my hand in your bag ... and you're going to stand over there like a good English gentleman. Right? (*kneels ... feels in bag ... jumps back*) Jesus! (*he holds bullets in his hand*) Fuck's this? What are ye doing with fucking bullets? Where's the gun? Where's the fucking gun? (*he points his gun in CASEMENT's face*) I'm going to fucking shoot you dead right now. Where's the fucking gun?

CASEMENT: There's a boat over there.

CONSTABLE: There's a boat? There's a fucking boat?

CASEMENT: A rowing dinghy. It's all completely innocent.

CONSTABLE: (*goes to CASEMENT and starts going through his jacket pockets, pulls out a ticket*) What's this?

CASEMENT: Let me see? (*the CONSTABLE holds it out*) Ah!

CONSTABLE: What is it?

CASEMENT: It's a railway ticket.

CONSTABLE: It's a funny fucking looking railway ticket. What does it say ... "eenweg?" Fuck's that?

CASEMENT: Einweg. It's a ticket ... one way ... from Berlin to Wilhelmshaven.

CONSTABLE: This is dated two weeks ago. You were in fucking Germany two weeks ago?

He cocks his pistol.

CASEMENT: Can I appeal to you as a fellow Irishman?

CONSTABLE: (*chuckles*) Go on. Just you fuckin try that, now.

CASEMENT: This is your country. It is both of our countries.

CONSTABLE: Are you a fucking Fenian? Or are you a fucking Hun?

CASEMENT: I'm a British subject. I'd like to speak to a priest... I'd like to confess...

CONSTABLE: Confess yourself to me, ye papish, Prussian bastard...

CASEMENT: I demand that you arrest me... I have the right to a fair trial and not to speak further in case I should incriminate myself. Arrest me. The charge is to be unlawful importation of armaments...

CONSTABLE: Is it? Is that what the charge is to be? Anybody who's that far up his own arse has got to be fucking English. You pick up yer fucking bullets, Mister Englishman. (*he puts CASEMENT in handcuffs and picks up the ball of paper CASEMENT had dropped*) I'm not some country cunt, ye know. (*CASEMENT starts to turn, the CONSTABLE stops him*) Walk, fuck ye!

SCENE 4

Scotland Yard, London: Easter Sunday, 23 April 1916

We return to the interrogation in the "present tense" and a repetition of the last action we saw from it. HALL smiles graciously and tears up his notes. CASEMENT is relieved. HALL smiles. He now has CASEMENT in his debt.

CASEMENT: You're very kind. I'm very grateful. Thank you.

HALL: Not at all.

Pause. HALL waits, quietly confident that this strange man will do all the work for him.

CASEMENT: I shouldn't want you to think ill of me.

HALL: (*blinks, startled again, then, smiling*) No ... why should I?

CASEMENT: I know I have much to fear. On my own account. I do know that. I know, I think, what a man like you must think of me. But I have done nothing of which I am ashamed ... except ... that I failed to do what I had meant to do. Had I done what I had meant to do, then this conversation would be taking place in very different circumstances. And it's the circumstances ... that I need to understand. Do you see? That's how you can help me ... to help you.

HALL: I don't follow.

CASEMENT: I need to know what's going on in Ireland ... today ... and until I do know ... unless you can tell me what is going on ... I don't know how much I can honourably tell you. It isn't for my own sake. I'm not protecting myself. I know that I am past protecting. It's other people I'm thinking of. I'm sure you appreciate that.

HALL: Well ... what other people? Who is it you're thinking of? Will you give me their names?

CASEMENT: (*with a bark of nervous laughter*) Well that's ... exactly ... what I mean. (*HALL waits, smiling*) If I were to tell you the name of someone ... anyone ... it may well be that this person hasn't done anything at all ... and I might get them into trouble. For no good reason.

HALL: And we shouldn't want that!

CASEMENT: No. I mean, I mentioned Richard Morten and...

HALL: (*barely able to disguise his amusement*) No ... I can see what you mean.

CASEMENT: So if I knew more ... of what was going on in Ireland...

HALL: Yes.

CASEMENT: It would help me...

HALL: Yes.

CASEMENT: ... to help you. I could ... disclose...

HALL: (*lightly*) Yes. But in the meantime – until we do know what's what! – and forgive me for asking you this again ... could you at least confirm your own name for me? I've got to write something down! (*he laughs in self-deprecation*)

CASEMENT: (*smiling, trying to be helpful, HALL having put him at his ease*) Officially, then ... I can confirm that I am Sir Roger Casement.

HALL laughs easily as he writes.

HALL: Good! Thank you! You're quite sure now? You are telling me that you are Sir Roger Casement?

CASEMENT: I don't think there can be anyone ... who should care to impersonate me. Do you?

They share a short laugh together.

HALL: I must caution you now ... Sir Roger ... and be sure that you understand ... that you are not bound to answer any of the questions I now put to you. But that anything you do say will be taken down and used in evidence.

CASEMENT: (*nods, then*) What is the charge to be?

HALL: You haven't been charged yet. But ... high treason ... I'd expect...

CASEMENT: I should ask legal advice.

HALL: Of course. (*HALL looks at him*) Are you feeling all right?

CASEMENT: Yes...why do you ask?

HALL: You're wet. You're sweating.

CASEMENT: Yes. I often sweat. It's a legacy of Africa.

HALL: Malaria?

CASEMENT: Yes. It's not serious.

HALL: You're sure? You don't need a doctor or anything.

CASEMENT: No, no. No, thank you.

HALL: So long as you're sure.

CASEMENT: I should ask ... to see a solicitor ... not a doctor...

HALL: Of course, but in the meantime ... merely as a matter of fact... (*he puts the ticket on the table*) Can you confirm for me that this is yours? A German railway ticket. (CASEMENT *doesn't answer*) You already said to the police that this was yours. What about this...? You dropped this on the beach. (*he shows the crumpled piece of foolscap paper to him*) It's a code key, isn't it? These figures here on the left...correspond to these messages on the right. "Await further instructions." "Send agent at once." "More rifles are needed." These are coded messages that you were to send ... to Germany. As and when the need arose.

Pause.

CASEMENT: Captain Hall...

CASEMENT *hesitates, unsure how to put this.*

HALL: Yes?

CASEMENT: I want you to understand... I'm not protecting myself. I'm not trying to be difficult... I'm not concerned with my own defence. I am quite prepared to answer all your questions in time, in the fullest manner, but only when I feel it would be right to do so. Which, at present, depending on the circumstances in Ireland, it may not be. Do you see?

HALL: (*showing him the code paper again with a little impatience*) This is your handwriting, though? Will you confirm that? (*CASEMENT makes no reply, HALL sighs*) We have many, many examples of your handwriting ... Sir Roger.

CASEMENT: (*looking*) Yes. Yes. It is.

HALL: (*holds out a black notebook*) So this is yours? You did write this in this notebook? (*reads*) "February 16th... Left Cork. Arrived Dublin 12 p.m.?" (*pause*) This is clearly in code. You weren't actually in Ireland in February, were you? (*insisting on an answer*) Were you?

CASEMENT: No. Of course not. (*HALL looks at him quizzically*) But it's not code exactly... This was written as an aide-memoire. Obviously ... the names of the places are not their real names ... but...

HALL: But not code names?

CASEMENT: It's hardly a cipher ... it's more of a stupid joke.

Pause.

HALL: Joke?

CASEMENT: Yes. (*HALL stares at him, not amused*) It's... That's just my diary. I keep diaries to help me remember things ... the names of the places are a joke ... to pretend to cover up the real names ... ironically. Like I'm playing at being a spy or something... I'm afraid you must think me rather childish.

HALL: You write jokes for yourself in your diaries?

CASEMENT: Yes. To remember. I like to remember things ... in my own way.

Pause.

HALL: (*reads*) "Wednesday 12th April. Left 'Wicklow' in 'Uncle Willie's yacht'?"

Pause. HALL waits as long as it takes.

CASEMENT: (*embarrassed*) It's just another joke. It's not really meant to conceal anything ... it's just a game. It's an old habit ... just for myself. When I hear someone else read it out, it sounds stupid. (*trying to explain*) I was alone in Africa and other places ... a good deal ... I needed to amuse myself...

HALL: "Thursday 13th 11 p.m. ... Willie's yacht broke down. Willie will need to give us another yacht?"

CASEMENT: Even if I interpreted that for you ... it wouldn't necessarily mean anything to you. (*HALL looks at him, expressionless, pause*) Sorry. I'm sorry.

Pause. HALL makes another note, controlling the pacing of their talk. He stops. Puts his pen down. Smiles sadly. HALL starts working on CASEMENT's regret.

HALL: Everyone was bewildered. When you turned up in Germany. At the beginning of the war. People were ... shocked.

CASEMENT: Yes. I can imagine.

HALL: I wonder if you can imagine how hurt people were. Everyone admired you. Everybody knew your politics, of course ... your support for Irish independence ... that's a perfectly respectable ... but to go to Germany!

CASEMENT: Yes.

HALL: You are ... or you were ... quite a considerable figure.

CASEMENT: Thank you.

HALL: A man of consequence ... with consequential friends. So ... now to be honest, it's a puzzle... We don't know what do with you. A well-connected ... considerable man like you.

Pause. CASEMENT fills the silence.

CASEMENT: Yes.

HALL: We knew that there would have to be some sort of reckoning with you one day. That's why I was assigned to you ... why I've been familiarising myself with your public and private life. But we didn't expect it would be till after the war that we'd be seeing you again...

CASEMENT: You were assigned to me?

HALL: Which is why you coming here now ... in wartime ... landed from a German submarine ... which is what I take it "Willie's yacht" refers to ... has rather taken us aback. Everyone. Both those who would have been disposed to be on your side, as it were ... and ... otherwise. If there is anyone ... if any remain loyal to you after what you've done ... biting the hand that fed, there are also those ... with louder voices ... in Parliament and elsewhere, as I'm sure you're aware – mainly Conservative and Unionist members from your own part of the world – who have been calling for your summary execution. Immediately. So ... in a way ... your being alive at all ... to hold this conversation with me is already something of a concession to a spirit of liberalism. (*smiles*) Quite frankly, we could have thrown your bullet-ridden corpse off the ferry before we got to Holyhead, Sir Roger, and hardly anyone would have shed a tear. So I do wonder, Sir Roger, if you are aware of the courtesy ... of this interview. I wouldn't have given much for your chances if you had landed from a submarine on a mission of violence ... in Germany, would you?

SCENE 5

Tralee, County Kerry: One day earlier, Easter Saturday, 22 April 1916

A church. A confessional. CASEMENT speaks to an unseen (or partly seen) priest.

CASEMENT: I haven't told the police who I really am yet.

PRIEST: (*while still changing*) Casement... Roger Casement... Yes... Now why is it I think I know that name...?

CASEMENT: Help me, Father. I'm trusting you.

PRIEST: What can I do for you, my son?

CASEMENT: Eoin MacNeill. He's a professor at University College... Might you be able to get word...?

PRIEST: ... Oh wait a minute, I know where I know you from... Are you not "Congo Casement"? Yes you are! You're that Congo fella... What's the name of that book?

CASEMENT: ... Professor MacNeill is the commander of the Irish Volunteers...

PRIEST: Ehm ... what was the name of it? That book with you in it?

CASEMENT: (*suggests*) *The Crime of the Congo?*

PRIEST No ... that wasn't it... That famous book...

CASEMENT: That... It was quite famous... It was written by Sir Arthur Conan Doyle...

PRIEST: Joseph Conrad ... his book...

CASEMENT: *The Heart of Darkness*

PRIEST: *The Heart of Darkness*. That's it ... that's the one... *The Heart of Darkness* ... up the Congo river ... to find Mister Kurtz ... dark and terrible man... The tortured natives ... slavery and madness... "Mistah Kurtz – he dead!" "The horror! The horror!" "Exterminate all the brutes!"

CASEMENT: Yes...

PRIEST: That was you, was it...? The fella who goes up the river...?

CASEMENT: ... well ... I did talk to Conrad about... I knew him ... in Africa. We spoke about ... conditions upriver ... in the ivory ... rubber ... concessions...

PRIEST: I'd always thought you were English...

CASEMENT: No.

PRIEST: No?

CASEMENT: No.

The priest laughs. Pause.

CASEMENT: He's Polish ... Conrad ... as it happens.

PRIEST: Well, is he? Is he now? What do you know? (*laughs, pause*) So, you want me to get word to the bhoys?

CASEMENT: Please ... if you can...

PRIEST: (*with a notebook*) What shall I tell them?

CASEMENT: I need you to tell them who I am ... that they should get word to Dublin... "There is no help coming. There is no help coming from Germany." It's hopeless. The Germans won't help. It has to be called off.

PRIEST: Oh... Now I don't know about that.

CASEMENT: Tell them ... please ... I failed. It's my failure. It's my fault. Please, Father...

PRIEST: Well... MacNeill in Dublin, you said?

CASEMENT: Yes. University College. Professor Eoin MacNeill. The Commander of the Volunteers.

PRIEST: Never heard of him. (*laughs*) Funny isn't it? Like I never knew you were Irish.

CASEMENT: I'm from the North.

PRIEST: Oh well ... the North. They let plenty of German guns in there ... for the Loyalists! Didn't they just!

CASEMENT: Yes. They did.

PRIEST: (*putting on his coat*) Casement. Casement of the Congo. You have my warmest admiration for all of the good work you did out there ... saving those poor black buggers... And now here you are in County Kerry! It's a small world. It's a much smaller world than we think. Isn't it? A smaller world than we think?

CASEMENT: Yes.

PRIEST: Well ... good luck to you. A great privilege to have met you. I expect we'll all be telling our grandchildren about this. Not that I've ... obviously... Do you have children?

CASEMENT: No.

PRIEST: Right then.

CASEMENT: Thank you.

PRIEST: Maybe there'll be a book!

Lighting change.

SCENE 6

Scotland Yard, London: Easter Sunday, 23 April 1916

We return to the "present tense" of the interrogation once more. Pause. HALL sees that CASEMENT is on the verge of saying something meaningful. He waits. Nothing. He writes, sensing CASEMENT is bursting to speak. CASEMENT eventually decides to come out with the question he has been burning to ask. He coughs. HALL looks up.

CASEMENT: Has anything happened today in Dublin? (*pause, HALL considers him, lets him sweat*) Please, Captain Hall ... has anything happened in Dublin today?

Pause.

HALL: Why? Was something supposed to happen? (*pause, they stare at each other, eventually*) No. All quiet. Nothing is happening in Dublin today.

CASEMENT can't conceal his relief. His whole body empties of tension. He becomes self-conscious, tries to laugh, then thinks he shouldn't. All the time HALL considers him coldly. CASEMENT settles. Pause. HALL drops one killing phrase on him at a time.

HALL: There was one thing... A Professor MacNeill ... who I believe is a particular friend of yours ... posted a curious announcement in the Irish Independent this morning, addressed to the men of the Irish Volunteers, cancelling today's "manoeuvres". Rather short notice ... I'd have thought. But probably for the best. The weather over there is frightful. It wouldn't have been much fun ... to do that kind of thing today.

CASEMENT: (*hugely relieved, partly at feeling able to confess*) Willie's yacht was a U-boat... We sailed from Wilhelmshaven ... not "Wicklow" ... obviously ... but the submarine broke down... I was landed by a replacement U-boat.

HALL: So Uncle Willie gave you another yacht, did he? (*pause*) You do understand, do you ... that what you've just told me amounts to a confession of treason? You're not still playing a game of spies?

CASEMENT: (*this being a moment for which he has prepared over and over again*) Oh, yes. I understand fully. I know exactly what I've done and what I'm doing now in confessing myself. I will not shield myself at all now. I accept in advance all the consequences of my actions on behalf of my country.

HALL: Your country ... is the United Kingdom of Great Britain and Ireland.

CASEMENT: No. It is not.

HALL looks at him with contempt, then writes.

CASEMENT: (*stung into saying more, getting more and more excited as he speaks, eventually standing, losing the place*) I don't expect you to accept it ... but I regard myself as a combatant on behalf of another country. Of an independent Ireland yet to be. You represent for me ... a Crown that I no longer acknowledge as my sovereign. All I ask

HALL puts down the paper. Picks up a sheet of A4.

HALL: This is an intercepted telegram ... from John Devoy in New York to you in Germany commenting on 12,000 dollars your Irish Brigade received from German sources...

CASEMENT: (*interrupting on "dollars", HALL talking over him*) That is a treacherous lie... You never believed that. If you intercepted THAT cable then you must also know that I immediately cabled back to Devoy to take legal proceedings in New York against anyone who published that libel... I never received one penny from the German government for the Irish Brigade...

HALL: (*interrupting on "penny"*) You came to Ireland on a U-boat. They gave you the use of a U-boat!

CASEMENT: (*talking over him, continuing from "Brigade"*) That is quite a different matter. That is quite a different question... I insisted ... if men were going to fight and die for Ireland then I had to be here too... I came home alone ... unsupported.

HALL: It is common knowledge ... that the German government has been providing for you. That Irish prisoners were intimidated, starved, offered bribes...

CASEMENT: (*heated*) Common knowledge has been misinformed. Not one of the stories you are telling me is true. Every man was a volunteer. There was no coercion of anyone. Every Irishman who had worn a British uniform and had been taken prisoner by the Germans was at perfect liberty... Every penny that I got in Germany for my work and sustenance came from my countrymen in America ... and I am proud to have had their support. Not one penny ... no help came to me from Germany... They offered me help ... they offered me money ... many times ... loans and grants and I refused them ... always ... because I knew that one day you and I ... or someone like you ... and I ... would be having this conversation ... and I knew when this day came my conscience would be clear. I have done nothing inconsistent with my honour. I am an Irishman. My country has no part in your war for your empire. It is oppression and injustice for Irishmen to be taken to fight for England and shed their blood ... and murder other men ... in England's war. It is not our war. Our war is for Ireland's freedom. That's the key to everything. Understand that and you understand everything. (*pause, HALL is writing, CASEMENT waits anxiously for a sign of understanding*) Do you understand?

HALL: Do you have a key ... by the way...?

CASEMENT: What key? To what?

HALL: To your rooms ... here in London.

CASEMENT: What do you mean?

HALL: Your flat. In Ebury Street? We shall want to search it.

CASEMENT: Break the door down. Break the locks on my writing desk. Break into everything. What do I care? (*going back into a speech*) I only ever did what I believed was right for my country!

HALL: (*pushing a paper to him*) Will you sign an affidavit to that effect?

CASEMENT: What effect?

HALL: That we needn't seek a warrant... It is the Easter weekend. Getting hold of a judge could be... It would save a lot of time.

CASEMENT: Of course.

He signs.

HALL: Thank you. (*inspects and puts away the paper, slightly bored now*) You were saying ... what you believed?

CASEMENT is brought up short by HALL's indifference, and becomes grander and more dogmatic in response.

CASEMENT: You don't care what I believe. I know that.

Do you think I've worked for you people all my life and I don't know that? No one in a position of power in this country cares what anyone believes except when those beliefs constitute a threat.

HALL: A threat?

CASEMENT: To the Crown. To the Parliament... To the flow of capital that runs through this great city like the river runs through it. To the complacency and self-regard of a nation that is barely conscious that its wealth comes from plundering the rest of the world. You are always in our minds ... but we don't exist for you ... except when we're dangerous. I do not think that anything is ever real to you ... except when your unearned privilege is in danger.

HALL: You believe yourself to be such a danger?

CASEMENT: Such is my hope. I hope I am.

HALL: Oh yes ... I'm sure that is your hope.

CASEMENT: It is my dearest wish to be exactly that which threatens Britain and her empire most. An independent Irishman.

HALL: And for the sake of that hope – of threatening "Britain and her empire" as "an independent Irishman" – you allied yourself with the Germans? Of all bloody people?

CASEMENT: I persuaded myself perhaps ... that the Germans were inspired by good will towards Ireland...

HALL: (*mocking, provocative*) Oh no? Not really! Surely?

CASEMENT: Some were, I thought. Others may have been simply ... seeking a military opportunity...

HALL: England's difficulty being Ireland's opportunity... Isn't that how the saying goes?

CASEMENT: That makes it sound ... mean.

HALL: It is mean. It is paltry. It is second-rate.

CASEMENT: History is not always dignified. It doesn't even necessarily choose the best people to make it. It's like the rest of nature. It selects from the material to hand.

HALL: And the hand of history selects you, does it?

CASEMENT: And you. You were chosen for me. Were you assigned to me because you're Scottish? Neither of us entirely fits the costumes history has chosen for us. I do know a bit about history. I made a little bit of history, you know? A long time ago. I was chosen to investigate a rumour, to put flesh on the whisperings that something dreadful ... biblical ... was happening in the Congo. I had the novel idea that if one wished to discover what was happening in darkest Africa then it might be a good idea to go and ask the Africans. So I did. And I made a little bit of history. It was my wish, of course, but it was also a combination of my experience working alone in Africa … and the fact that my superiors never quite knew what to do with me. It was an accident. History only looks like it was meant to be that way afterwards. It's not like a story at the time.

HALL: We'll never know … will we? What history would have made of the two of us sitting here chatting so pleasantly if things had worked out differently. If you and I were sitting talking here … while a German army set your island "free".

CASEMENT: What does freedom mean to you, Captain Hall?

HALL: It is that of which you have just deprived yourself, Sir Roger.

CASEMENT: (*smiles*) That's a pragmatic description.

HALL: I'm a naval gunner by training. I deal in practicalities. Calibre. Range. Closing speed. I'm hesitant about using words like "freedom" just for the important sound they make. I fear that it is all too easy to persuade yourself … that just to say the words is to make them true.

CASEMENT: But who is to define "self-determination"

and "freedom" Captain Hall, if it is not those who have determined to be themselves ... and to be free? Whoever attained any of these things, without acting as if they were already true? As if they were already free and already every bit as good as everybody else.

HALL: You weren't ever going to Egypt, then? We had reports. About your Irish Brigade going to fight in Egypt?

CASEMENT: (*scornful*) No! I'm afraid that's another story you got from unreliable sources. The Germans talked about the struggle for liberation from the British Empire ... in Africa ... but...

HALL: (*smiles*) But they have an African empire of their own...

CASEMENT: Indeed they do. They have an African empire. Like England does. Like France ... like Belgium, like Portugal... I know them all. I was twenty years in Africa, Captain Hall.

HALL: Yes. You served there with great distinction.

CASEMENT: That's just it ... that's what you don't... That's the gulf in understanding between us. I didn't "serve". I was just like those Irish soldiers in those camps in Germany. I didn't serve ... out of duty or love. I was bought and paid for. By shipping companies, by ivory traders ... by King Leopold of the Belgians ... and then by the British Colonial Office... I was bought by the British Crown. I may talk like a gentleman, Captain Hall. I may be able to do that impersonation. Like you do. My school ... like yours ... may have been just expensive enough for that. But despite what you may think of my "connections", I am the product of a declining provincial middle class. I needed a job. I needed money. And your empire is where all the money was.

HALL: There was more to it than that. There was more for you in Africa than that.

CASEMENT: Yes. Of course there was. The best of me ... is still there I think. (*he laughs quietly*) You've arrested a ghost.

Lighting change.

SCENE 7

St George's Square. Pimlico: Some hours earlier on Easter Sunday

The telephone is ringing in HALL's flat. He goes to answer it.

HALL: Good morning, sir. Yes, sir, thank you for calling.

I appreciate... (*listens*) Yes, sir, quite prepared. (*listens*) Well, yes, sir ... I'm afraid so. On the face of the evidence... (*listens...frowns*) Well ... if he were to decide to cooperate, then ... we could... (*listens*) Of course I'll remind him, but... (*listens*) Well ... no ... no, sir ... with respect ... I don't expect him to ... so... (*listens*) Well... No, sir ... I don't think he is. No. (*listens*) Well ... yes... That argument may be open to him medically, sir... But ... I'm sure. Casement's immoderate, certainly ... romantic, yes ... but... (*listens, laughs politely*) Yes, sir. He is Irish, that's... (*listens*) Yes. I do understand that the world is watching. (*listens*) I don't believe that I am prejudiced. No, sir. (*listens*) Is that a suggestion, sir... Or is that an order? (*listens – that was a step too far, he backtracks*) No, sir. Of course not, sir. Of course, I appreciate all you've done for me... "The quality of mercy"... Yes, sir.

The call ends. HALL slowly puts the phone down. Lighting change.

SCENE 8

Scotland Yard, London: Easter Sunday, 23 April 1916

We return to the interrogation. HALL has made CASEMENT a cup of tea. They are "on a break".

CASEMENT: (*for the tea*) Thank you.

HALL sits. He smiles.

HALL: It may seem like a hundred years ago to you now ... but you were decorated. Twice. You were honoured by the king. You were received by the highest in the land.

CASEMENT: Yes.

HALL: You were very grateful at the time. It isn't that long ago. Five years? I have a letter here that you wrote to the Foreign Secretary on the bestowal of your knighthood ... that's ... effusive.

CASEMENT: When you break into my flat, Captain Hall ... you will find a trunk in my bedroom cupboard. At the bottom of the trunk there is an unopened package sent me ten years ago ... containing a medal naming me as His Majesty's Companion of the Order of Saint Michael and Saint George.

HALL: You didn't deserve that honour, then...in your opinion?

CASEMENT: Every penny and every honour I received from the British Empire was a betrayal of my country. My serving you there ... and my ... rewards for that service ... estranged me from my own people.

HALL: And that justifies your turning on us, does it? After all the honour that the British Empire has done you?

CASEMENT: It was a commercial arrangement, Captain Hall. Not one of love. I'm sorry to disabuse you.

HALL: Did it affect you otherwise? Africa?

CASEMENT: I learned in Africa that if human beings are deprived of their rights in where they live, if the land that they stand on belongs to someone else, then nothing else will compensate them. I understand Ireland through Africa. And Africa through Ireland.

HALL: I mean did it affect your mind?

CASEMENT: In what way?

HALL: The jungle? Malaria?

CASEMENT: It may not seem that way to you, but I believe I'm in my perfectly right mind. I believe I am saner now than I have been in thirty years.

HALL: (*shrugs*) Still... You might consider insanity. As a defence?

CASEMENT: How dare you?

HALL: I'm offering you disinterested advice, Sir

Roger. You're going to find yourself in an English courtroom where they think Irishmen are all mad anyway. Perhaps if you were to blame the whole thing on malaria?

CASEMENT: Why are you insulting me? Why are you doing that?

HALL: I'm not.

Pause. CASEMENT smiles defiantly.

CASEMENT: I'm not mad. I may seem that way to you. But I'm not. (*HALL writes*) You can call me anything you want. You can accuse me of whatever you like. You can't provoke me any more than my country being part of your empire is already a provocation.

Pause. HALL has tried to offer CASEMENT an escape and he's been turned down. He moves towards a summing-up.

HALL: So ... the Germans weren't serious ... they weren't committed to your cause... You failed to make history? You are humiliated. That's your word ... not mine.

CASEMENT: Yes.

HALL: That's your story?

CASEMENT: Yes.

HALL: So how do you explain the ship?

CASEMENT: Ship?

HALL: The guns. On the ship. All the guns. On the German ship in Dublin Bay. The Aud, I think she was called. (*checks his information*) Yes. The Aud. We picked her up yesterday. With 20,000 guns in her hold.

Pause.

CASEMENT: Yes.

HALL: You knew about that, did you?

CASEMENT: Of course.

HALL: And how does the practical matter of 20,000 German guns fit in with your mission of peace ... of eventual happy reconciliation between our nations? (*CASEMENT hesitates*) I'm particularly keen to hear you answer that question.

CASEMENT: When you examine those weapons, you will find that they are barely serviceable. Antiques.

HALL: Antiques?

CASEMENT: Breach loading ... no machine guns ... no artillery... And far, far too late... If the Germans had been really serious in supporting a rebellion, those arms would have needed to arrive months ago ... for training, for... That arms shipment is more of a gesture than a practical contribution.

HALL: 20,000 guns?

CASEMENT: Yes.

HALL: A gesture?

CASEMENT: Yes. I finally understood ... they were just using us...

HALL: Using you?

CASEMENT: Yes ... it's why I insisted I come separately ... by submarine ... despite the discomfort...

HALL: I don't follow...

CASEMENT: They betrayed us. They led us on. They never meant us to succeed.

HALL: The Germans?

CASEMENT: All they wanted ... was a massacre... All they wanted was for us to rise up ... and for the English to have the embarrassment ... the shame ... of putting us down. Their support of my efforts ... was fraudulent... They were using us ... and the moment I understood that ... the moment I understood what they were really doing ... I made up my mind ... to come home.

HALL: They used you. They made a fool of you.

CASEMENT: If there were to be fighting in Ireland, I had to be there, yes? I had to be part of that... I had to be there ... but I dissociated myself ... from them ... from those arms ... that deception... I wanted no part of that ... treachery...

HALL: You practise very delicate discrimination in treachery, don't you, Sir Roger? You "dissociated" yourself?

Lighting change. CASEMENT relives an encounter with a German officer just before embarkation.

CASEMENT: No. I want no part in it. I won't do it. You're using us! You pretend to help us just enough to get us to do your dirty work ... and when they come down upon us for their vengeance, you will be nowhere to be found. You will abandon us, abandon my boys, to their fate. You don't want Ireland to be free at all, do you? All you want is chaos! All you want is blood. You want them to massacre us. Don't you? You want them to be disgraced and you don't care how many of us die for the sake of their embarrassment. Well, I won't do it. I won't take part in your masquerade. I refuse to let you take me or any of my boys aboard that vessel. I shall not have it said that I handed a hundred Irish boys over to the hangman. It is reprehensible. It is dastardly. It is theatre!

HALL: "Willie's yacht"...

CASEMENT: Yes. Just three of us ... that's all ... we left the others behind... I saved them...

HALL: Were you then close to the Irish coast?

CASEMENT: No ... we were one day only at sea, we ... turned back.

Lights return to "natural" state.

HALL: It's like a comedy. Everything went wrong. You made a hopeless hash of everything. Is that what happened? Is that what you're really telling me? That you're a fool? Is that what you're asking me to believe?

CASEMENT: I have done ... many foolish things.

HALL: (*close to him*) Has it occurred to you ... because it occurs to me ... on this short acquaintance with you and with the facts ... that the first German submarine did not break down at all ... that the Germans were trying to stop you getting to Ireland ... and cocking everything up?

CASEMENT: I don't know what they were thinking ... how on earth would I know...

HALL: You're in a better position than anybody else to guess.

CASEMENT: It doesn't matter. Nothing matters. What they were thinking or what I was thinking or what you're thinking of me now. The uprising is prevented. And no Irish blood will be uselessly shed.

HALL: Or British blood... No thanks to you.

CASEMENT: (*exhausted suddenly*) I'm still glad I came home, though. I'm very glad that I came home, even for a moment ... that I breathed Irish air, as if it ... and I ... were already free. As if ... I enjoyed that. That was good.

HALL stops writing. He gets up and sits on the table close to CASEMENT, making one last attempt to bring him back into the fold. This is intimate. It is insightful. It nearly works.

HALL: You have gone to great pains in the course of our conversation ... to identify yourself as an Irishman. Now, it sounds to me ... as if you were trying to persuade yourself. Because they don't trust you, do they? The Irish. They don't believe in you. You're "wrong" ... you're from the wrong tribe ... you don't fit... You're a Protestant ...

you're Northern ... you spent your life working for the hated British Empire... You were knighted for your services. So to the Irish, you're one of us. You're a traitor. By birth and by experience. It's very clear ... from the correspondence we intercepted from the Irish in Boston and New York ... that they think you might well be a spy. But our spy. A British spy.

CASEMENT: In any colonial situation, suspicion and division are a tool of the colonising power. I know who I am. I know where my loyalty lies.

HALL: Do you? Do you really know who it is you serve? Are you really going to hide behind simple-minded, nationalist clichés? Don't you think more of yourself than that?

CASEMENT: The complexities ... of who I am ... or who I might be, who you are ... who anyone is ... are simplified in time of war.

Pause. HALL rises, impassive, and comes round the table to make his final pitch ... to CASEMENT's loneliness.

HALL: The Germans didn't think much of you either. I speak as a professional in these matters. They abandoned you ... on a beach ... not knowing where you were ... alone ... without false papers, without support, without contacts, without an address to go to. With nothing ... but this ludicrous code. (*HALL gets very close, very seductive*)

There was no one there to greet you. No one there to help you...after all of your work ... after all that you've dared. All that you've lost. They left you for dead. They left you to us ... so why are you protecting them? These cowards who have betrayed you to your solitary fate. Who've called off their "manoeuvres". Who are skulking in hedgerows in Kerry and in dark pubs off Abbey Street singing their old songs and feeling sorry for themselves. Give me their names, Sir Roger. What loyalty do you owe to them compared to what you owe to us?

CASEMENT turns away. HALL turns CASEMENT's head to face him, touching him for the first time.

HALL: Who are they? Oh, there's no need to fear for them. We are not your Huns, we are not monsters like your rubber planters in the Congo and the Amazon... We do not act without the law... We do not prosecute men for their opinions no matter how repellent. We do not care what a man believes provided he believes in private or in peaceful conclave. We are not indifferent to belief ... we will engage in debate like the civilised, civilising people we are... But we will not have treason. We will not have guns. We will not have murder done in the name of Ireland any more than we will do murder in the name of England... Because above all else ... England stands for the law. (*very close, intimately*) We have our own list of suspects. You must know we do.

And that there isn't a name that you could give us that we don't already know. You may've hanged yourself thirty times over ... but you know that if they are innocent, if they have committed no act of terror, they will have the protection of the law. I had hoped ... that you, as a gentleman ... as the man of honour that you claim to be ... would have had the personal generosity of spirit to relieve some of these deluded men of our suspicions ... to clear their names ... spare them the wrath you have called upon yourself. (*holding his face*) You're alone. You're alone. You're as alone as any man anywhere has ever been.

CASEMENT: It would be dishonourable. You can see that. I may sacrifice myself to you. I may not sacrifice them.

HALL looks at him. He decides that he is done with him. He has tried unsuccessfully to win further disclosure, but now needs further instructions and information. Abruptly he resumes his seat and begins putting his papers away.

CASEMENT: Are you finished? Can I go now?

HALL: Am I finished? Can you go? (*closes his briefcase*) I'll make my initial findings known to my superiors and await more instructions. We'll resume this tomorrow afternoon. You'll be taken to prison now.

CASEMENT: Which one?

HALL: Does it matter? Brixton, probably.

CASEMENT: So that I can tell my people. My family. I have fifty pounds ... it's tied in a bundle ... where we hid the boat. If it's not been stolen. For expenses ... for a solicitor.

HALL: We'll find it. We'll pass it on.

CASEMENT: Thank you.

HALL: Till tomorrow then. I hope you get some sleep.

HALL exits. CASEMENT goes to lie on the bunk. Blackout.

SCENE 9

Montage: That night

CASEMENT is lying on a bunk in his prison cell. He remembers Africa. Meanwhile, HALL breaks into a trunk from which he takes CASEMENT's medal and a set of black notebooks. He settles on a chaise longue in CASEMENT's London flat and begins to read. We hear a montage of voices belonging to HALL, CASEMENT and a third voice, that of a young West African woman, ELIMA, making a statement to CASEMENT on his journey into the interior of the Congo in 1904. This is accompanied by projections of contemporary images.

ELIMA'S VOICE: I heard the firing of the guns. I ran out with my sister. My brother ran away by himself. As I ran I heard my mother call me, but I told her to run the other way to find my brother, and I would stay with my sister. My sister was heavy so I could not run fast. Many people passed me. I left the road and went to hide in the bush. When night came I tried to find the road again and follow the people who had passed me, but I could not find the road. We were in the bush six days.

CASEMENT: Go on, Elima.

ELIMA'S VOICE: One of the soldiers who found us said, "We might keep them both, even the little girl is not bad-looking," but the others said, "No, we are not going to carry her all the way." So they put a knife through my sister's stomach, and left her lying where they had killed her.

ELIMA is too upset to continue for a moment.

CASEMENT: Please. It's important.

ELIMA'S VOICE: When they took me back to town, all the people had run away. They found only one woman, who was dying of sickness, and the soldiers killed her with a knife. At several towns they found no people, but at last they came to a town where several people had run to as they did not know where else to go. At this town they killed a lot of people – men, women, and children. They cut the hands off those they had killed, and brought them to the white man to show him how many and for him to pay them money. When they went home, the hands they had cut off – they just left lying, because the white man had seen them, and counted them.

CASEMENT: What happened then? How did you escape?

ELIMA'S VOICE: I was two weeks at Bikoro with the soldiers then I ran away into the bush for three days, and when I was found I was brought to Chief Misolo and he asked me why I had run away. I said because the soldiers had thrashed me and raped me. Mr Clark the missionary was with Misolo and Mr Clark took me here to the mission station at Ikoro. I learned that my mother had been killed by soldiers and my father starved himself to death because he had lost his wife and children.

CASEMENT: Thank you.

ELIMA'S VOICE: Did I do well?

CASEMENT: You did very well.

ELIMA'S VOICE: It is a shameful thing to tell.

CASEMENT: It is much more shameful ... if nobody knows...

Lighting change. HALL reads excerpts from CASEMENT's diaries. This is accompanied by projections of contemporary images of gay life.

HALL: (*he reads*) After dinner out to Bella Vista and round plaza. Some splendid Indian lads with huge ones and beautiful sterns and tried with several. Finally coming home a young soldier, thickset Inca Indian and gave cigarettes and three shillings and he accompanied me. Mine up and he looked and would have done it.

25th Wednesday. Young white soldier talking to others in shirt, open bosom and knickers and put one hand on his and he showed enormous extension ... they all gathered round and looked. It was lying down, thick and about seven inches. In afternoon lovely green-eyed boy of twenty. He has a huge, soft, long one. I saw it plainly on left side loose pants. He smiled and bowed. I love him.

Also one of the carters, a big Inca with blue shirt and pants and a perfect monster. It swings and shows a head about three inches in diameter. He has enormous shoulders and curved strong back, as strong as a stallion. He has a lovely gentle face.

Three o'clock. Waiting for Jose, my fly open.

Stayed till near five. Got stiff and fingered it. Mine up and I pulled it and he got redder and his very big. After dinner to band and saw lovely boy. Tuesday going home.

SCENE 10

Scotland Yard, London: The next day, Easter Monday, 24 April 1916

HALL sits waiting at the table. CASEMENT comes in in handcuffs. He sits, expecting the handcuffs to be removed. They aren't. HALL is writing.

CASEMENT: Good afternoon, Captain Hall.

HALL looks up. Stares blankly for a moment. He then smiles professionally.

HALL: Good afternoon, Sir Roger. I've been instructed to begin this afternoon with a technical question. Are you in fact a British subject? I know that you're "Irish", of course, but Ireland, in this instance, has no legal existence, you understand?

CASEMENT: I don't follow.

HALL: If you committed your "act of war" upon the

United Kingdom as a subject of the German Empire then we could treat you as a prisoner of war, do you see?

CASEMENT: Captain. I am your defeated enemy. You can do with me as you wish.

HALL: (*laughs*) Oh, if wishes were horses, Sir Roger ... beggars would ride.

CASEMENT: You'd have me shot, would you? Without further inquiry? If the choice were yours? Is that your wish?

HALL: Did you become a German citizen?

CASEMENT: Why are you asking me a thing like that? You know better than that. (*HALL waits, CASEMENT sighs*) Albeit reluctantly, Captain Hall, I remain a British subject.

HALL writes. Pause.

HALL: You're on your high horse today, aren't you? Did you sleep better?

CASEMENT: Very well, thank you. I dreamed about Africa.

HALL: One often finds ... that on arrest, the criminal sleeps. Relieved, I suppose.

CASEMENT: No ... it's just on the U-boat I never slept at all. Brixton prison is comparatively comfortable. Might I repeat my request for legal representation? I've had no contact with anyone.

HALL: Maybe nobody wants to talk to you. Maybe they're all ... disgusted. (*CASEMENT now looks at him warily*) Yesterday I asked you to provide me with the names of your ... what shall we call them? ... fellow conspirators. You withheld those names on the grounds of their inaction yesterday.

CASEMENT: What's happened?

HALL: I thought I would try something different this afternoon. I thought I would give you some names ... and see what you could tell me about them.

CASEMENT: Captain Hall ... what has changed...?

HALL: Thomas J. Clarke. (*CASEMENT is silent*) Lord! This again! (*tries the next name*) Seán Mac Diarmad...da? Is that how you pronounce it? (*angrily*) For goodness' sake! It's an innocent question!

CASEMENT: MacDermott. It's the Irish form of John MacDermott...

HALL: Do you know him?

CASEMENT: I'm not going to answer that.

HALL: P. H. Pearse? (*CASEMENT is silent, HALL is angry, suppressing terrible rage*) Who is he?

CASEMENT: These are public figures ... you don't need me ... to tell you who they are.

HALL: I'm ignorant. I'm a stupid Scotsman. Save me a little time.

CASEMENT: Pearse is a schoolteacher. He runs an Irish language school.

HALL: A schoolteacher?

CASEMENT: Yes. (*HALL writes*) What is that paper you're reading those names from?

HALL: (*spells out*) C ... E ... A ... N ... N ... T? Cunt?

CASEMENT is shocked. Scared.

CASEMENT: Kent... Again ... it's an Irish form of the name.

HALL: Éamonn Ceannt?

CASEMENT: Captain Hall....

HALL: James Connolly?

CASEMENT: The trade unionist.

HALL: Joseph Plunkett?

CASEMENT: What is that paper?

HALL: Do you know Joseph Plunkett?

CASEMENT: I know him and his father. They're very well-known people... Please.

He holds out his hand. HALL gives him the paper. CASEMENT reads, increasingly horrified.

HALL: This schoolteacher of yours was parading in Sackville Street half an hour ago. Declaring the Irish Republic. As several hundred armed men occupied the post office and three other places in the centre of the city... (*HALL quotes ... actually paraphrases selectively*) "... supported by her gallant allies in Europe, Ireland strikes in full confidence of victory."

CASEMENT: (*to himself*) Oh God. What have I done?

HALL: You must have thought you were being so fucking clever. All day yesterday! With the stupid Scotsman. Making a fool of me. It was all called off, you said. You just came back to call it off...

CASEMENT: I did...

HALL: (*ignoring him*) You were just a harmless fucking lunatic... And then today, when you had lulled us into slumber, when our garrison had all gone to the Curragh for the races...

CASEMENT: No ... I...

HALL: The damned Irish, on the one hand despising us and all we stand for, and on the other trusting that our decency will prevent us from wiping them off the face of the earth.

He knocks CASEMENT to the ground. CASEMENT reaches into his pocket for a pill which he brings towards his mouth ... but HALL is too quick for him and rips the pill from his hand.

HALL: What is this? What the fuck is this? (*he throws the pill aside and picks CASEMENT up*) Do you think you can make a fool of me?

CASEMENT: I refuse to answer any questions. I demand that you immediately provide me with legal representation...

HALL: Who do you think you are? What do you think this is? (*he locks the door*) I told you yesterday ... that you are alone. That was not quite the whole truth. You are alone ... with me. (*he picks CASEMENT up and pushes him against the wall*) Yesterday, you led me on a merry fucking dance. Today is another day.

CASEMENT: Keep away from me ... take your hands off me...

HALL: Are you scared? Are you scared of me? You're a soldier, aren't you? You're ready to fight and die for Ireland? Well, come on and fight me! What are you waiting for? Come on! I'm right here. Why don't you fight me for the sake of the aul sod? (*offers his chin, then, with contempt*) I know why you don't fight... (*he throws the black diary to him*) Look! Look at this. I've read it. I've read your fucking diary. (*he takes the book from CASEMENT, leafs through it*) You won't fight because you're fucking queer ... you're a half-dead, used-up, groping, squalid old bumboy who pays real men to suck him off. You're not just a traitor to us ... you're a traitor to your sex, to nature and to God. Christ ... I wouldn't be you ... not for all the tea in China.

He laughs. He seems to relax a little. CASEMENT tries to engage with him.

CASEMENT: Captain Hall...

HALL: Shut up. Christ, you make me sick. There is nothing about you that doesn't make me sick. When you were out there in those jungles being a friend to all the niggers, were you paying them to fondle your floppy Irish dick? Were you hanging round the public toilets in Berlin corrupting German soldiers? How many of your Irish Brigade are fucking queer as well? Did you bumfuck your way across the North Sea in that long hard fucking U-boat? (*CASEMENT tries the door*) Where the hell do you think you're going?

CASEMENT: Captain Hall, no purpose is being served by this interview.

HALL: This isn't a fucking interview. I don't see any fucking lawyers in here! Just you and me.

CASEMENT: I am entitled to protection as an enemy combatant...

HALL: No you're fucking not. You're not a Brit, you're not a Kraut, you're not a Mick ... you're not even a man. You're stateless. You're nothing. You're a corpse. You're a terrorist. You're a nonce.

CASEMENT: I have no information for you. I am as surprised as you are by the events that have transpired in Dublin today...

HALL: I don't care. You and me are done with history. There's nothing left but bodies. Fight me. (*he slaps CASEMENT*) Fight me.

CASEMENT: You're mad. You're insane.

HALL: Too fucking right I am. (*he picks up the declaration*) You and your band of schoolteachers have just unleashed hell. You're about to get an education in hell's geography. You just changed the fucking rules. While all you people did was write pamphlets and folk songs, we could treat you like children. But now you want to play around with overthrowing British rule ... with guns? What the fuck did you expect we were going to do?

CASEMENT: What you're doing. We expected you to do exactly what you're doing.

HALL: Well, I'd hate to disappoint you. (*HALL punches him expertly in the midriff, CASEMENT goes down*) There. Did you like that? Is that what you wanted? Is that the kind of thing that you enjoy? I've got some more if you enjoyed that.

CASEMENT: Don't ... please...

HALL: (*mocking*) "Don't ... please..."

HALL hits him again. After a minute, HALL picks him up.

HALL: Let me tell you a wee something. My youngest brother died at Ypres last year ... for you. Whether you wanted him to or not. And now ... you are going to die for me. (*hits him again*) My brother Johnny was killed at a place called Hill 60. It was the first gas attack made on White troops. You know that the Germans first used poison gas on Africans, don't you? On French Zouaves from

Senegal? Well, this was the first time they'd used the fucking stuff on our people ... and my brother and the rest of them didn't know what was happening. The shells landed almost silently ... they broke like eggs ... and there was a smell like a swimming pool... And then there was choking, tearing, burning in the throat and lungs ... men ripping out their own necks in fear and agony ... a rolling, invisible fog of horror ... horror ... creeping across the hill. That's why we can't forgive you ... we can't indulge you. No matter what we want to do... No matter how merciful we want to be. That's why it doesn't matter in the end that you're an Irishman or a hero, or a poet or a homosexual or a knight of the fucking realm. They died ... my brother died ... thousands of men have died ... and are going to die ... so we can't let you live. To spare a thing like you ... would be monstrous.

CASEMENT: You're in the navy. Why aren't you on a boat?

HALL: (*decides to ignore that*) Maybe we'll give you a trial ... maybe not. Maybe they'll just drag you out of your cell one morning and put a bag over your head, shoot you and feed you to the crows. I don't know. It doesn't matter, does it? We're already so deep ... so deep in horror. It's too late... No matter how they squirm ... up there ... my superiors ... with their consciences, no matter what we think later when we've had time to think about it, it won't be in time to save you. It won't be in time to save those deluded fuckers in that post office. Because you're right. Actually. All of us are going to do exactly what we always knew we were going to do.

CASEMENT: Why did they assign you to me? Why?

HALL: I feel sorry for you. Because I know what happens next. When I unlock that door, they'll take you to the Tower of London. It's where we keep our traitors. We've had hundreds of years of practice at this. They're going to take you there, and they're going to put you in a wee room on your own. You won't know if it's day or night, but they'll keep the light on all the time so it won't make any fucking difference. And time will pass ... acres and acres of time will pass ... in silence ... with you just sitting there in your growing stink listening to your heartbeat slow right down until it stops.

CASEMENT: It's not because you're Scottish, is it?

HALL: (*angrily*) You're going to miss me. Do you know that? You're going to long for our wee chats. You're going to beg for someone, anyone to talk to you. Even if it's just to call you a dirty Irish pervert.

CASEMENT: Captain Hall, does everybody know that you're queer?

In a blind rage, HALL beats CASEMENT.

CASEMENT: Yes! Yes!

HALL lets him go, disgusted. CASEMENT leans against the wall, recovering. Eventually, he goes to the sink to wash his face.

CASEMENT: You're not my first, Captain. You are by no means the first "real man" of my acquaintance whose reaction to his state of arousal is to lash out at the object of his desire. I have been beaten before. (*CASEMENT sits, HALL sits not looking at him, eventually*) I really didn't mean for anyone to read my diary. I didn't leave it lying around with the thought of anyone reading it. I'd ... forgotten about it. There are some homosexuals ... for whom the superficialities of our sexual lives are themselves essential for arousal ... for whom criminality is stimulating. I am not one of those. While I may not be proud of all of its manifestations, I do not hold my nature itself to be something of which to be ashamed. I'm older than you ... perhaps my acceptance of myself is a function of my greater experience ... you may never share that perspective. But I don't find your guilt exciting or interesting either. I decided, years ago, to live as a homosexual man in the same way I decided to live as an Irishman. As if it were all right. As if it had no consequences... As if it weren't complicated to be who I am ... or as if the complications that it might cause for other people ... were their affair, not mine. I didn't advertise it ... but I refused to conceal it. I decided that the only way I could become free and the equal of anybody else was to act as if that were already the case, as if Ireland were already free, as if ... it were already all right ... for me to be myself.

HALL: I spent all day yesterday ... trying to save you. I was under orders ... my instructions were to find a way ... to help you find a way ... to save yourself. But this will break you. It will destroy you. Any residual sympathy for you as an Irishman, or as a servant of the empire, or as an advocate for the rights and dignity of suffering humanity ... all that ... will be swept into nothing by the disgust and embarrassment. They've made copies. For circulation, at first, among the service chiefs and senior government ministers ... and then, of course ... the American ambassador, senior figures in the church ... the Catholic Church as well as the Church of England. I have an appointment ... for lunch on Thursday ... at the Carlton Club ... to meet with the editors of six national newspapers, and two American papers ... all of whom might have been expected to plead for clemency in the matter of Sir Roger Casement ... but now ... they will walk by on the other side. How could you be such a fool? As to allow us the use of a weapon like this?

CASEMENT: What does it matter? I came home to die.

I should have died years ago. I should've been shot by that policeman on Banna Strand. You should have let me eat that pill the Germans gave me. I'm used up. The best of me is a spirit ... haunting a glade in Africa or a glen in Antrim. I've no business being alive here with you. I'm sorry you didn't let me die.

HALL: Oh ... we'll let you die all right. But hasn't your bloody country got enough glorious dead already?

CASEMENT: Apparently not yet, no. (*pause*) I'm sorry that your brother died. For your country.

HALL: He didn't die so much as he retched his guts inside out ... for two unbearable months. His death was ... a blessing. But it's kind of you to say so.

CASEMENT: I did the right thing. I believe that.

HALL: Your German friends exterminated a whole race of people in your beloved Africa ... did you know that? The Herero. It was the Germans' dress rehearsal for ruthlessness ... for their racial superiority expressed in violence.

CASEMENT: I know.

HALL: You know! You know everything! Look at you. Sitting there in your righteous Irish peace ...

protected by the grave you've dug for yourself... all confessed and shriven and shiny. And vain ... you're such a piece of vanity. What will they think of your penchant for oversized cocks in the Catholic Church? What do you imagine this "Free Ireland" of yours will have to say about the lineage of self-regarding sodomites you people go on about? Alexander the Great? Leonardo da Vinci... Roger Bumboy Casement? Do you imagine your legacy as a homosexual hero will fill the history textbooks of Holy Mother Ireland?

CASEMENT: I don't imagine we'll be perfect.

HALL: It is quite possible, you know ... with discretion ... for a gentleman to exercise his preferences in almost perfect security. It is the likes of you, flaunting your affliction like some sort of flag ... who manage to mess things up ... for everyone. You and Oscar Wilde ... declaring yourselves as evangelicals for Ireland, Art and Buggery ... that's not what I call self-determination. That's self-indulgence. Still, with luck ... when they throw your body in the limepit, that will be the end of your revolting clamour for recognition ... of your nationality and of this sexuality of yours that you insist we look at. Everyone's alone. Don't you know that? We live and die alone.

CASEMENT: I won't be alone.

HALL: Oh no ... of course ... all the saints will be

with you. Ireland's martyrs will stand beside you on the scaffold. Good God, man ... aren't you above all that nonsense? Once upon a time, you were very nearly an Englishman.

CASEMENT: Like you?

HALL shushes him. Tuts, waving his finger. He goes to exit. He turns.

HALL: I shan't be seeing you again. What I'm going to do now is play my part in the destruction of Roger Casement. It's not something I'm especially proud of. But it's not something of which I am ashamed.

HALL unlocks the door.

CASEMENT: Captain Hall... You've done your duty. You have been exactly the servant to His Majesty ... that His Majesty requires.

HALL: And when you're safely dead ... you will be exactly the kind of Irishman of whom Ireland can be proud.

CASEMENT: Would you like me to forgive you?

The two men share a final laugh. HALL unlocks the door. He exits. The door is locked.

SCENE 11

Statement at the Old Bailey, London: 26 June 1916

CASEMENT: If true religion rests on love, it is equally true that loyalty rests on love. The law that I am charged under has no parentage in love. I am being tried for the offence that as an Irishman, I loved Ireland first.

Loyalty is a sentiment, not a law. It rests on love, not on restraint. The government of Ireland by England rests on restraint, and not on law; and since it demands no love, it can evoke no loyalty.

Self-government is our right, a thing born in us, a thing no more to be doled out to us, or withheld from us than the right to life itself – than the right to feel the sun, or smell the flowers, or to love our own kind. I am proud to be a rebel, and shall cling to my "rebellion" with the last drop of my blood.

SCENE 12

Tower of London: 3 May 1916

CASEMENT, *dishevelled, filthy and starving, is*

on a bunk. He doesn't look up at any point. A Welsh SOLDIER stands in the dark beside and behind him. The soldier doesn't look directly at CASEMENT when he speaks. CASEMENT doesn't raise his head when he replies.

SOLDIER: I do wish you'd eat something. You look terrible. Like one of those bloody women getting porridge in a tube.

CASEMENT: You're not supposed to talk to me.

SOLDIER: Where's the harm? (*pause*) I probably shouldn't be telling you this either, but they started shooting them today. Those fellows from the post office. You should see the photographs. Dublin's in a hell of a state. Looks like bloody Belgium ... all the houses with their roofs burned off. What did you silly sods want to go and do a thing like that for?

CASEMENT: Who's been shot?

SOLDIER: Oh, I couldn't tell you their names ... but these chaps have been in front of tribunals, and now they're getting put in front of firing squads.

CASEMENT: (*paraphrasing Pearse*) "The fools. While Ireland holds these graves ... Ireland will never be at peace."

SOLDIER: I'd think not. Silly sods. (*looks at him briefly*)

And what do you think you're doing? Starving to death for Ireland? I shouldn't bother. They'll probably blow your head off tomorrow.

CASEMENT laughs briefly. SOLDIER laughs briefly. They are both silent. Blackout. The sound of the scaffold's trap crashing open as CASEMENT hangs.

people are together in this world is a dress rehearsal for Hell ... when we will be stuck with one another permanently, listening to Andrew Lloyd Webber.

(smiles)

But I'll be back at school tomorrow. Like you'll be back at work, or pottering in your woodshed, or at the shops ... or whatever it is you do. And Isobel will be wherever she is.

We go back. That's what we do. We go back. Like nothing has happened. Nothing has changed. There's nowhere else to go. No one to be but ourselves, no matter what face we wear. Nowhere to go but back to where we started. We're alive. And that's what life is.

And it's all right. Isn't it? It's all right.

(she sits)

You never know, do you? Who is sat beside you. You don't know what their story is. You don't want to know. Why would you? That's fine. I'll just sit here.

(pause)

Suppose I did speak. What would I say? Look at my face. What do you think I'd say?

head propped up to look comfortable, so empty of everything, as if she'd never been ... as if she had never been there... I saw her scooped out, hollowed out, eviscerated. That's what I saw. I didn't see the arrival of peace, I saw the murder the universe commits every day, the war it fights against us, the war that we can't win. She didn't look peaceful, she looked beaten, defeated.

She looked like the dead, empty face ... of almost everything. Almost everything out there ... in the universe ... is dead.

That's why life is so precious. So fragile ... because it's so ... vanishingly rare.

She's gone ... Mum's gone ... that changes everything. It takes me back to when we were children, when everything seemed to be a war between us. And now, you don't even want my face.

(pause, she smiles at them)

How can people stand it ... how sick we are of each other at the best of times? How can we stand the sound of one another's voices, when the sound of our own is so unbearable? How can anyone stand to hear what anybody else thinks ... when our thoughts trip out after each other as obviously as zombies?

You go to pubs and clubs and the Edinburgh Book Festival and it all feels like death, like everywhere where

Why does it matter so much?

It must be life, mustn't it? It can't be anything else. What we see in each other is what we're going to lose one day ... it must be life ... and that is why we feel things together, if we do ... it's why we love. It's why it really matters to me that Andy Murray wins a tennis match or Fischer-Dieskau sings Schubert or Alfred Brendel plays Beethoven ... or that my mother died ... that this thin, tenuous, deluded activity ... life ... is over.

After her last stroke, when I came in from the airport ... so distraught, so angry with myself ... with Isobel ... when I came into the room ... Mummy's eyes opened for a minute and she looked at me, I knew it was not me she saw. There was not enough of her left to recognise me, or my voice, or my shape or my face. Or to see at all. Yet I had the illusion ... from her face ... that she knew me. The illusion of life.

Her desperate fear at the sound of my voice ... as her chest heaved and bucked her on the bed ... her eyes ... looking at me, not seeing me, not seeing anything or recognising anything. I was still reading recognition into a face behind which the brain was so radically damaged as to make any but the most basic animal responses impossible ... was she alive then? In any real way? My mother? Our mother...

You didn't see her face dead, Isobel ... her body a symmetrical lump beneath a blanket on a slab ... her what my mummy didn't think I would know what to do with.

Isn't that terrible? Money. This is all about money. Isn't that ... second-rate? But I couldn't face her ... so I went to the library instead ... and I couldn't face the library ... so here I am.

That's the truth. And the truth maters, I think ... though it's unfashionable to think so. The truth matters. More than happiness ... more than anything.

Why am I even telling you? What expectation can I have, scientifically speaking, that you will even understand that? I am a scientist. I do understand my own objective and subjective relationship to the facts of the universe on the one hand, and to the fact of me being me ... a universe unto myself ... on the other. And so I ask myself, I ask you ... here, now ... truthfully, scientifically... Is there really anything we can really share? How can any of us even ever talk to each other and expect to be understood? How can I ever know that you feel what I feel? To put it another way, why is a dead body so dead? What is it that was once present and is now so brutally, finally absent? Is it because the change from alive to dead is so terrible, so shocking and profound, that when we look in their dead faces ... faces so blank and hateful now that they are stripped of love, now that we can no longer read them, now that we can no longer feel our own fears and hopes reflected in those eyes ... that we feel that something like the soul is gone away?

It's my face. It's my face you're saying isn't good enough. That's my life you're having surgically improved. My facial hair, my cheekbones ... me.

(she becomes aware of the audience, laughs)

I'm all right. You don't need to look so worried. It's just that today, the lawyers were winding up the estate ... and it brought it all back ... the helplessness ... the chaos of my feelings last year ... like stripping off a sticking plaster and finding the wound is still angry. Because yes ... Mum left Isobel everything. Everything. Because Isobel would know what to do with it ... that's what Mum said in her will. That's the will that was executed today.

Last year, when the will was read ... Isobel wasn't even here to hear it. She ran away to Dubai the moment the funeral was over. She sent Gavin along to hear ... and pass along the news ... that she had got everything. The house, the investments. All of it. She laughed. Gavin told me. She laughed.

And I could hear Mummy laughing. Everybody laughing.

I could have challenged it, of course. The lawyer told me that if I challenged the will, I might still inherit up to 25 per cent ... less his ... cut ... He licked his lips at the prospect. I swear he did. And today I was supposed to meet Isobel to talk about the estate, now that it's been "executed". I was supposed to meet her ... and beg ... beg her to pay me my share of little theatre of the dead they have in the basement of the hospital ... and left me there ... it took me a moment to recognise her. She was so ... dead ... on the slab, a pillow underneath her head. Why do they do that? What's the pillow for? The pillow was for me, not her. To make it look like this cold lump of meat was sleeping. At peace. It was a lie. I felt sick. I hate lies.

I was thinking on the bus back into town that every relationship I have with everyone is going to be different now. I was terribly angry with everyone. That's why when the young man came down the stairs of the bus letting huge Irn-Bru burps emerge from his chewing mouth ... I wanted to kill him. To tear his throat out and ask him as he lay drowning in his own blood, "Why would you shit on the world if not for the pleasure of your own smell?"

I wandered around talking to myself for days after Mum died, wondering if I would ever be all right again. I heard what I said to myself and it sounded a bit crazy. I knew it wasn't really me ... it was my grief. Refocused unreasonable anger is one of things grief does to you. It says so in *Good Housekeeping* magazine. So I said nothing to Isobel ... of course ... except to myself. I didn't call her on the phone and scream at her. I sent my feelings round my own body instead. Round and round. By tighter and tighter cancer-producing pathways.

(*angrily*)

when Isobel was with her and I was on holiday ... the first holiday I'd had ... for years ... I had to admit it to myself ... I'd already given her up, I think. I had given her up. I'd been with her so much towards the end that when it came to the very end ... the truth is ... the truth is ... that despite what I told myself ... I'd had enough ... I'd had enough and I left them to it. Her and Isobel and the Liverpool Care Pathway... So I wasn't there again ... just like with Granny. I wasn't there. I'd left the room again. Maybe that's why I'd gone on holiday in the first place. Perhaps that's what I was doing.

Anyway, she died a year ago and I wasn't with her ... so by myself ... out of guilt, probably, I asked to see her body in the morning. I never told Isobel I was going in like she'd never told me about the hospital phoning. Seeing her was just for me.

I don't really know why I did that. It was too late to say goodbye to her. Did I want to see the reality of her corpse? As a punishment? She would not be watching me from Heaven, I knew that. She'd not be any more or less conscious of me than she was the last time I saw her ... when her torn-up brain could do no more than tell her lungs to gasp like a tortured robot and her heart to pump oxygen to a skull that was already a useless, dead stalk, and all I could do was wipe her mouth and listen to the tearing growling in her chest.

When they took me through the curtains ... into the

Isobel was with her ... for once ... when she got ill again... I was away, you see... I was on holiday... And Isobel didn't call me. I suppose she might have thought that was the kind thing to do. Maybe the hospital advised her. The health service manages death for the living as well as for those who die.

I was angry ... when I found out the next day ... of course ... and of course I flew home ... it cost me a fortune ... and I was going to be so angry with her... I was looking forward to being so angry with Isobel, all the way home ... but then, when I thought of the white lie I told Mum when *her* mother was dying, I couldn't really be angry with Isobel, could I?

I told Mum that I was in the room with her mum ... Granny ... when Granny died. The truth was that I was in another room. The truth was that maybe they took advantage of my being out of the room ... to give her a little push. The truth is that's maybe why I left the room. Because I wanted them ... just a little ... to get it over with. I never told Mum the truth about that. She asked me at the time and she asked me again recently, when she knew she was dying soon too. Had I seen Granny's soul go up to Heaven? When Granny died. She held my hand tight ... and asked me to tell her I'd seen Granny's soul.

And I said ... I said, "Yes, Mum ... of course I did."

So when Mum went into the stroke unit that last time ... a year ago ... when she had the second stroke to everyone. So you go to cognitive therapy. So you can feel good about yourselves. And write books about the joys of getting to know the real you, hiding inside of you, the real beautiful, childish, selfish you. Books which you sell to people who are just as desperate and childish and selfish as you are.

"This is my time," she told Mum and me... "I'm making time for me." And Mum seemed to believe her. Mum told her she was right. Mum wanted ... to do everything for her. "Why not, Isobel? Why not live for today? What does it matter?" If what we are is what we want. If we are all desire, then we're not real. We're ghosts. Behind our faces.

(suddenly angry)

It's my face. This is my face. These are my years. This is my life in my face ... my laughter, my tears, my loves, my losses ... my loneliness ... it's my face. Me. This is me in my face. What is wrong with this face? Why do you want to have this nose and these cheeks broken and reconstructed? What is wrong with this face? Every lie, every insult, every missed opportunity, every failure to gain promotion ... they are all written here. This is my writing. This face is my book. It says, "I will not live in fear. Of other people, or of poverty, or illness, or of loneliness or of time. I am not afraid. I am not afraid to grow old. I am not afraid to be alone and poor. I am not afraid of the truth. I am not afraid of who I am. I am not."

about five years ago. That's what Gavin thinks made her discontented. But she must have been unhappy already ... mustn't she? And she did have a history of depression. And she's not depressed any more. Oh, no!

Cognitive therapy is all about exploring yourself. Who you really are. What you really want. And who you really are always seems to really want to burn a huge hole in a Marks and Spencer's credit card. Then get somebody else to pay for it. Well, if there is no God any more to tell you different, then there is nothing wrong with anything, is there? It's all just opinions, isn't it ... one opinion is as good as another? If you lack the remotest capacity for moral reflection, nothing is wrong with anything.

I think this is why the terrorists want to blow everything up. I don't think they're mad. I think they've got a point. I sometimes think they're right. I know that there have been times in the household items aisle in Asda ... when if I'd had a suicide belt with nails in ... I'd have quite HAPPILY...

What's wrong with me? Hmn? Why don't I like the world? Aren't I one of these comfortable, educated people, all at liberty to go out and find ourselves at aged sixty ... and go to interesting places, and get cognitive therapy... Why does it feel so wrong to me? Maybe it isn't only me it feels wrong to? Maybe it actually feels wrong to everyone? Does it? Is that why you all go to your therapy and your exercise classes? And the pub? Because life feels wrong. It feels wrong problems is to buy things ... maybe the commercial dimension of it all just reflects reality. Perhaps that's who we really are? We really are a society of second-rate hippies ... fancy-free ... self-determining ... maybe that's all right too. Maybe this is the freedom that all of our struggles through all of history have been for. This is why the Pankhursts chained themselves to railings. And got force-fed through a tube.

It's what everything's all about now. This is a world of old people with money ... and old people without it. Self-indulgent whores in hotels in Dubai, sunbathing on sculpted islands, and old men dying in falling-down libraries full of madness and stink. That's the story of the twenty-first century. That's the story of Isobel and me. She has always had everything ... she threw it all away ... and now she's got even more. And I've got nothing. Just this face. I've only got this face.

(pause, looks down, recovers)

And she is nice, really ... Isobel. If I think about it dispassionately. If I get outside my anger and look at her. She's not Hitler. She's what we call a nice person. Like everyone we went to school with ... It wasn't at all like the school I teach in, the school we went to. It was a nice school for nice girls, and we are all grown up now and comfortable ... and still reasonably well mannered ... so what's wrong with that? Really. What is actually wrong with that?

Isobel started going to ... knowing yourself therapy ...

she got ... everything she ever wanted. She is spending her children's future. On this bloody man.

(she looks at an audience member)

You'd do that, would you? If you got the chance. If your husband was foolish enough to sign over the house to you? Would you?

Why not? Haha! Why not?

If a woman feels she has another fifteen or twenty years of active life ... why not? I mean, the only real reason women didn't used to do things like that is that they were so shagged out... People live longer, healthier lives now ... maybe that's all there is to it... And they think, these women with health and money, "The kids will be all right, they're grown up" ... and you don't want to think about nursing homes, do you, when you're only sixty ... and you think ... why not? It's the kind of thing you see in the magazines all the time. Middle-aged woman, in a rut, goes off to the sun to rediscover ... or indeed, discover for the first time, that she is a free and attractive agent ... in the pond ... attracting all the fish. Then writing about it in the magazines. And the *Daily Mail*. What's wrong with that? Even the women who can't afford to do it secretly really want to ... don't they? And just because what they really want seems to be an uncanny match for the advertisements and lifestyle consultants in the same magazines ... doesn't make it wrong. Even if it is a bit suspicious that the answer to all of life's little enough for her any more ... now that she has found herself...

I don't imagine she'll do so much laughing in future. Her face might fall off.

And she left him. Gavin. After thirty-two years. She just upped and went to Dubai ... for a "trial separation" ... to see if she "liked it" ... to see if she "liked herself that way". Of course she did! She loved herself! So then she told him she was leaving him for good. Leaving their children ... me and Mummy ... everything!

Gavin is still in bits. He has always adored her, always indulged her. He still does. Even now. He did everything for her. He gave her the house. He let her keep the car, he moved into a flat with their son, Clifford... Gavin's sixty-three. She ... we ... are sixty years old... People our age never used to do things like that. Can you imagine our parents doing a thing like that? Our grandparents? Apparently there's lots of them now. Nice, middle-class ladies of a certain age ... all kicking their husbands out for no reason at all and going off to find themselves ... like Bette Davis in *Now, Voyager* ... you remember ... but as if it was Bette Davis's mum who went on the cruise ... had a bit of a nip and tuck ... then met Paul Henreid.

And she has, of course. She's met some man out there. In his forties. And she's spending ALL the money ... Gavin's money ... Mum's money, even before the estate was settled. Before she even got it. Even before

It is possible that my straightforwardness has sometimes not been good for me.

There are those in the staffroom who call me humourless, for example. A soor ploom, I think I overheard one day. A miserable cow another. I don't deny that some people, many people possibly ... find things funny that I don't. Obvious, crass things. But I do not feel the lack of caterwauling or laughing like an idiot at the slightest mention of flatulence. Which is why no one who ever knew us in any substantial way ever mistook us one for another, my sister and myself. No one who knew us at all well ever thought that she was me or I was her. Isobel has always enjoyed a fart joke.

"Can't you be more like Isobel, Morag?" ... my mother used to say as I was putting her to bed. "You're so serious." "Yes, mother, I am serious," I would tell her. "I am also here. Isobel is not here ... dressing you and cleaning you and feeding you. Isobel is never here. She is away somewhere. Laughing at both of us."

And that was even before she went mad. Even before the cognitive therapy. Even before she decided she had to have the surgery. Yes. The surgery ... of the elective, plastic variety.

(touching her face)

A cut here, a lift there. Her nose broken and reshaped, her cheekbones ... her laughter lines ... and she was always laughing. None of these features ... are good all places. Not to discuss the performance. To discuss "it". Mummy's money ... now that the estate has been ... liquidated ... is that the legal expression? But I couldn't face her. I just couldn't face her. So I'm here instead. Facing you.

There is a performative aspect to schoolteaching, of course there is ... but the subject that I teach ... basic science, mathematics ... to secondary school pupils ... is not theatrical ... it is not about me or my opinion. My opinion of their beauty does not affect the chemistry of phosphate bonds one tiny little bit. The world is what it is, eventually.

I do not like to talk about myself. I do not always understand people. I do not understand, for example, why anyone thinks that there is anything resembling music in the works of Andrew Lloyd Webber, but I am prepared to let that go. I am prepared to concede that there must be songs for people who don't like music ... theatre for people who don't like drama, just as there is literature for people who don't like reading, and painting for people who don't like art. And that there is television for people who don't like anything. I understand and I forgive these things. I am, generally speaking, very positive on the subject of people ... if you put them in context. And remember that they stink.

At the same time, I will not be underhand. Dishonesty is not something I will contemplate. So when I tell you that my sister is a whore, and she has gone mental, I am not being strategic. I am telling you the simple truth.

They didn't press charges ... the shop or the police ... but they came to the school. The police did. And Mrs MacKay called me out in front of the assembly. Can you imagine? Of course ... I didn't say anything. I could have ... I could have blamed Isobel ... she was always the one who was in trouble. But I didn't. Of course not. So I stood there quietly. Saying nothing. In front of the whole school. To be admonished.

(*pause*)

I would never normally talk to strangers like this. I don't like to "share" such things... Everyone knows that when I speak, I don't speak lightly ... so when I called my sister a stupid selfish whore on the telephone last time I spoke to her, with Mummy's lawyer listening, I meant exactly what I said. She is a stupid, selfish whore, and this man she's met out there is an utter hound who will ruin her life, which is all that she deserves, but she should be thinking about other people. It is other people she is hurting too. I was not play-acting with her ... every word was torn from the root of feeling. She laughed at me anyway, down the line from Dubai ... like she always does, like always ... thinking I'm like her, thinking that I am calculating, performing my indignation, using it as a bargaining tool in the matter of Mum's estate... She thinks that my emotion ... emotion like this ... is something you turn on and off for your advantage. Like an actress. A whore. Like her. As if I were like her. I'm not like her. I'm not.

We're supposed to be meeting now. In a theatre of

I remember how I discovered her "journalism". I was at the doctor's. There had been a mix-up on Mum's prescription and I was waiting for Mr McKeve to sort it. So I picked up a copy of *Hello*. I wouldn't normally ... and there were all these vacuous, airbrushed faces of all these appalling people I'd never heard of who were all rich and famous for some reason or other, and I flicked over the pages ... and there it was ... my face. Well. I thought it was my face. Of course it was Isobel's face ... on her byline... She had her own byline...

I read the article. It wasn't good ... but it wasn't bad as these things go. And for a moment ... I was proud of her... She'd told me nothing of her ... journalism ... and just for a moment ... I flirted ... I caught myself pretending ... just for fun ... that I was her. That I'd written it ... that the world was interested to hear my thoughts ... I was daydreaming, obviously...

(pause)

Sometimes, when we were younger, she pretended she was me. When she did something she shouldn't have. She was actually caught shoplifting once. In John Menzies. And she gave them my name. Can you believe your own sister would do something like that? Not just picking up a handful of Sherbet Fountains and stuffing them up her jumper ... but getting caught ... with sherbet all down her ... and then saying that she was me. The calculation involved in doing that. I think she'd already made her mind up she was going to say she was me if she got caught... Seven years old.

I am not an old ruin. I am gainfully employed. I am not a sponge on the state. I am not an alcoholic. I do not start the evening with a bottle of sherry, then go the pub till I can toddle off home for a vodka... I am not depressed ... or "mental".

Of the two of us, it is my sister that has gone "mental". It is not me. I want that very clearly understood. We are twins. But we are very different people. She is married. I am not. She has children. I do not. I have had a career ... she has had a succession of wee jobs to keep her occupied. She does things for charity. I work for a living. She and Gavin and the children have been everywhere and seen everything. He is a nice man ... a little dull ... but he works very hard and has done very well ... but five years ago ... my sister Isobel "found herself"...

And since she has "found herself" through the marvels of cognitive therapy, she has been publishing little self-satisfied gobbets of banality in women's magazines ... about pottery and kitchens, fracking and farming, and "finding herself", of course ... about all of which she knows exactly nothing...

Exactly nothing being apparently the exact amount of content of an informational or philosophical kind that is required by women's magazines ... and now she's working for the *Daily Mail*...

(pause)

genotype. But I don't need people. I do not require validation. I do not need to be told who I am. I do not need to see my reflection in the eyes of others so that I can see myself. I rely on myself and find myself to be reliable.

I sometimes wish I was the kind of person who could wear T-shirts. Just so that I could have a T-shirt made that says, "Do I LOOK like a fucking people person?"

My sister Isobel on the other hand ... has always been a people person, as she says herself... She has always been surrounded, making herself available ... and especially now   since she has "found herself" ... since she has "found herself" and made life miserable for everybody...

(pause, she smiles.)

I do still teach, actually. I certainly can't afford to retire. Science. Yes, I'm a lady science teacher and that is still quite unusual. You're right. There's nothing as queer as folk. How very true.

So I am still working, if that's what you were wondering. People do wonder, I should think. Middle-aged woman ... on her own ... in a pub. Alcoholic ... that's what you might think. If you were unkind.

He just wouldn't stop coughing. I can still hear it.

Yes, I'm a teacher. At the end of her tether. The end of her disappointing, unfulfilled tether ... that's who I am. I am that cliché.

I didn't know him. I never know any of them. Even though they all know me. It's like being a minor celebrity ... being a teacher... I go about sometimes and I catch sight of these slack jawed idiot boys and slutty idiot girls chewing gum and texting each other ... "Isn't that old beetle jaws?" ... and I say to myself "Yes ... Yes, it is I. Beetle Jaws."

I do not go and say hello. I do not mind their stink of fear and failure. I do not mind the noise of their second-rate minds. But even when I was their teacher, I never pretended I was their friend. Because I hate lies. The mendacity of such a posture appals me ... and it is so obvious ... your pupils despise you for it.

If I don't relish contact with strangers like yourselves, it's not because I suspect you, although I do suspect you stink ... morally ... no offence ... but because you will suspect me of wanting something from you ... when I don't want anything. I don't want anything from anyone. I am happy with nothing, thank you.

Which turns out to be just as well...

I am not uncomfortable with human contact as such, even with humans with whom I clearly have nothing in common but our remotely shared ancestral and tighter until we get cancer... Or lash out ... just ... lash out.

(aware of being strange)

I know what it's like. You go out for a quiet drink or a cup of tea somewhere and suddenly some stranger sits down and starts talking to you about their life. And your face just freezes into a pretend smile, doesn't it ... just like that? Just like you're smiling at me now. You know what your smile says? It says "please don't hurt me. I'm Scottish."

I'm not going to hurt you. I've never hurt anyone. I've never hurt a fly. I've always tried to be good. I am decent to everyone. Even when they're obviously just pretending to be decent themselves.

People stink, actually. People just stink. Like that man on the bus burping his Irn-Bru ... he came down the stairs of the bus just burping repeatedly and staring at me slack jawed ... unshaven. Mouth hanging open. Burping. Why would you do that, you wretched little man? Why would you deliberately set out to make the world uglier? Why are you doing that to me today?

I wanted to ... slap him. The way he looked at me ... I wondered if he recognised me ... if fifteen years ago he had sat flatulently at the back of my "Introduction to Science" class.

and ask him. "Why are you alive?" What good is it doing anyone to be reminded of all the filth and corruption we carry inside? I felt sick.

Well, they're free and they're warm, aren't they, libraries? So they're bound to be full of poor, mad people. There's nowhere else for poor, mad people to go these days, is there? To cough and be disgusting in. No one goes in to read a book. How could you? Like no one ever went into phone boxes ... when there were phone boxes ... to use the phone ... if the smell was anything to go by. And if you weren't poor already you'd never put up with it. I mean, trying to read while that noise is going on. People are disgusting, don't you think?

(provocatively)

Poor people, old people, sick people. Are revolting.

(she looks at them, challenging)

We just don't say that kind of thing, do we? Scottish people. We have a particular brand of social hypocrisy that makes us SAY that we don't mind people being mad and poor and ugly in theory ... but we run a mile in real life, don't we?

We never feel anything properly. Whatever it is ... grief ... or anger ... or pain ... it doesn't seem to matter what it is ... we bottle it up, we send it round our insides ... round and round and round ... tighter

I don't know why I even wanted to come in here. I'd no intention of talking to anyone, but sometimes one just wants to hear other voices.

(looks at them looking at her)

It's all right. You don't need to worry about me. I didn't just escape from anywhere. It's been quite an upsetting morning, that's all … and I needed to go for a walk and...

(recovering, smiles, changes the subject)

I was in the library just now. I'd forgotten what they were like nowadays. I'd not been in that particular library since I was at school. Isobel and I were both at school near here.

They are such awful places now … aren't they? Well mebbe you never go into libraries. They're not what they were. And it's not just the books. I don't mind the books so much, though they age badly and they smell peculiar. It's the people. Who age badly and smell … disgusting.

There was this old chap sitting behind me. The smell of old sweat would have gagged a horse. He just wouldn't stop coughing. And it wasn't the cough so much as the liquid in his lungs, gurgling and bubbling and him sniffing and swallowing and coughing it back up again. Like he was doing it deliberately. "What is the point of you?" I wanted to turn around good about it... I can do the wrong thing and not feel guilty at all. Why shouldn't I have plastic surgery? Why shouldn't I wear any face I want?

(she sits, looks around for MORAG)

Where IS Morag? When IS this bloody play supposed to start?

ACT 2

A sixty-year-old woman makes her way to a seat in a pub, apologising as she does.

MORAG

Forgive me. Do you mind if I sit here? No, please ... don't let me disturb you. I'll just sit here quietly.

There's something wrong, isn't there? I don't look the type, do I? Oh I might come into a pub with my husband if I had a husband. And he was a bit racier than me. But I don't have a husband, do I? You can tell.

I thought you might think that I was my sister Isobel. We're identical twins, you see, and I thought that you might think... She's quite weel kent ... as they say... We have the same face.

and wrong isn't difficult ... it's only playwrights who think that right and wrong is complicated ... and yet ... and yet...

Will I?

Here I am, at this moment ... free, happy ... rich. I'm rich. I have real choices. Never mind the bullshit governments and retailers feed you about choosing between fifty-seven varieties of second-rate crap... I have REAL choices. And I like it. Why shouldn't I like it? Isn't ... freedom ... like this ... real freedom ... what human life aspires to, what human life is supposed to be... I'm healthy and wealthy and I can afford not to be wise!

I have reached, absolutely accidentally, the very pinnacle of what all human life should be. What everybody wants. No matter what pious bullshit they feed you. What every commie, every Buddhist, every hypocrite wants... Freedom from want and fear of want ... freedom from fear. I can live where I want and how I want. Anything I want to eat or drink, anywhere I want to live, anywhere I want to go with the possible exception of space... This is the paradise that preachers postpone until you die ... and force you to be good for ... this is the utopia that communists and anarchists die for ... this is what terrorists wake up for in Paradise ... when they've blown themselves up for Allah ... and I've got it ... here and now. It's mine. I can do what I want... I can do the right things or the wrong things ... and feel

And I wasn't surprised. I wasn't surprised at all. Don't you remember the day I came to see the two of you when I told you I was leaving Gavin? "At last," Jennifer had said ... "At last." "What about poor Gavin?" you said. "Well if you liked Gavin so much, Morag, it's only a bloody pity you didn't marry him," I said. And Mummy laughed. Do you remember? She laughed. And she said "I did." Like that. "I did."

You didn't know what that meant, Morag... So you dismissed it like everything else that your scientific brain doesn't understand ... but I understood. Daddy ... dear Daddy and dear Gavin... She had married Gavin too. She had been married to a man who had disapproved of her.

She told me all kinds of things after that. About the men she had. The secret affairs. Your hair would stand on end. You never understood her at all.

So anyway ... I wasn't even there when Mother's will was opened ... like they do ... but I wasn't surprised she'd left everything to me. The house, the properties, the shares ... everything... Because "Isobel will know what to do with it" ... and poor Morag ... humiliated ... after all she'd done ... after all her sacrifice ... when Gavin, horrified, phoned and told me ... well I couldn't help but laugh and laugh and laugh...

And of course I'll share it ... half and half ... of course I know that that's what I should do. Right girl. I know he was ill ... but he said it... I know he was in pain ... but he said it...

I showed you. I showed all of you. It's me now, with a column in the *Daily Mail* telling all of you what to think, me with a readership of thousands, me who can crush people with a word, end careers with a shrug and mock you ... mock you for your pretensions and your consciences. It is my opinion that is sought and paid for on anything from immigration to summer fashions to the prospects for the royal baby ... it is my superficial, stupid, expensive opinion. And my opinion, for what it is worth ... is that everyone is selfish, everyone does everything because they want to ... and yes, Morag, that includes you being the one who scraped the shit off mother's sheets all those years ... and don't think Mummy didn't know it. Of course she had to tell you you were good because you so desperately wanted to be good, you had always wanted to be good ... but she liked ME. Mummy liked ME!

It wasn't my *fault* that Mummy enjoyed my visits. It wasn't my fault that Mummy liked it when I took her out to hotels, when I reminded her of what it was to be young and happy. It wasn't my fault that Mummy liked me making her feel young more than you making her feel old. Everyone is attracted to energy. It wasn't my fault that you were away on that trip when she died. And it was not my fault, Morag ... that Mummy left me her money. Because Mummy knew, Morag ... that I would know what to do with it.

It was awful... It was awful for everyone. But for Morag ... it was all a plot ... and the victim, as usual, was her... I couldn't deal with her so the minute after the funeral I went back to Dubai ... and the superficial Tony... I didn't even tell him what had happened, poor shallow lamb – he couldn't have remotely coped ... so I didn't tell him anything and we went to bed for a week...

Everybody is selfish. Morag is a scientist. She ought to know that. She should know that people only do the right thing, so called, because they want to. They do it because it pleases them, and it pleases some people to be martyrs. Morag chose to sell her little flat and to move in with Mummy when Mummy had the first stroke. But she was there anyway. She was alone anyway. It was actually closer to the school. And she was so proud of herself. It gave her pleasure. It gratified her to lord it over me. Of course, as twins, there was always going to be a bit of competition for affection and so on ... for approval ... and Morag always thought she won. Yes, I was the popular one – because I wanted to be popular – at least in part to compensate for her being so clever, and so evidently, so grossly unfairly Daddy's favourite and it was all because of that bloody music ... that bloody music that went on for days that they pretended was so deep and so spiritual ... when for me ... for me ... it was punishment. It was reproach. It was pain that I deserved because I found it so painful ... because of my "superficiality" – Daddy used that word. He said that I was a selfish, superficial empty-headed little woman had been filled full of electricity ... bucking, backward and forwards ... like a robot ... but breathing, impossible deep breaths in and out, mechanically, like she was an athlete or she couldn't breathe. Brainstem stroke ... they told me ... catastrophic brain damage...

And I didn't tell Morag. I didn't tell her that night. I missed one phone call when I was at the hospital with Mum that first night ... and she called me later on on the mobile ... and I was in the hospital car park ... and I decided not to tell her ... after all ... she still had *Götterdämmerung* to come...

I didn't want to spoil the holiday for her. The first proper holiday ... she'd allowed herself since Mum first took ill ... so by the time she called the next time ... I'd already agreed that Mum be put on the Pathway ... be kept comfortable ... and that's all. There was nothing they could do. The damage was too severe ... so I told Morag ... on the Saturday morning... So Morag came back ... she never got to Vienna ... and she came to see Mummy, and she hated me... She was so angry with me... She had spent all this time with Mummy and I had ... swanned over for three days and I had killed her ... like she had finally trusted me to play with her toy and I had broken it...

When the hospital called the house early on Monday morning ... Morag was asleep. I didn't see any reason why I should wake her.

thought that's what I was doing. For years, Morag has wanted to go to Vienna ... and Bayreuth... She's wanted to make the gloomy pilgrimage to the land of Mordor where the dark lord broods over great big chords and plodding baritones. And she found this package on the Internet ... two weeks in Vienna, Salzburg and Bayreuth... So I said, "Great, I'll come and stay with Mum." And she looked at me as if I were going to come and set fire to the house or get drunk and leave her on the potty all night ... and it took me a month to persuade her ... but finally off she went.

And Mum and I had the jolliest time ... we really did. We went out for walks ... we got her buggy stuck in the mud on Mugdock moor ... we had a laugh ... we had a couple of bottles of Prosecco ... and I did all the cooking and cleaning like a good girl ... I didn't call in my daily woman more than once. And that was to deal with an accident ... you know ... and eventually Morag even stopped phoning every night in the interval between the fourth and fifth act of *Siegfried*...

And anyway ... Mum had the stroke ... the second stroke ... the one that killed her ... she had the stroke on the Thursday night the first week Morag was away... She'd been asleep in her chair, quite the thing, after what she told me was the loveliest cheese omelette she'd had in years ... and she woke up ... and said "oh"... Oh ... just quietly, like that ... and something happened ... it was like this quiet little

And there she was looking after Mummy and I wasn't looking after anyone, I wasn't looking after Gavin or my children... I was being looked after ... like some reject, like some defective duplicate of her ... with the same face... And nothing seemed to help... I suppose that medication "levelled me out" ... but ... five years ago ... and don't laugh ... five years ago I discovered cognitive therapy. I know, it sounds awful to our Presbyterian, self-reliant, Scottish ears ... but I discovered in behavioural ... tricks ... in acting as if I was happy ... that I became happier...

So I told Gavin I needed a break and I went somewhere sunny. I went to sunny places. I took what Gavin offered me and I went to Venice, I went to Istanbul... I liked it so I lived there for a month, overlooking Galata Bridge. Then I met Tony and we went to Dubai. And Tony was fun ... he wasn't deep, he wasn't improving, but he was forty-two years old and he fucked all night. I know, shocking. But after thirty-two years of half reluctant fumbling ... Jesus ... it was good ... it was like in one of those films ... it was like *Awakenings*, like Robert De fucking Niro coming out of a trance.

And do you know what Jennifer said ... when I left Gavin finally after thirty-two years ... my darling, fantastic girl who I'd felt so guilty about neglecting when I was ill ... she said, "At last." That's what she said. "At last!" Because she understood...

I thought I was giving her a break... I genuinely

of falling in love with him... I was going to leave them all then... But then Gavin and Jim sat down together ... and I don't know what happened... Jim avoided me ... until I saw the "For Sale" sign going up in his garden ... and I felt ... used ... betrayed ... like dirt...

I thought I was dirt... I thought everybody and everything hated and despised me and I thought they were right...

God this is so long ago and it still upsets me...

... and Gavin looked at me so sorrowfully ... so disappointed in me ... so faithful and true and strong that I wanted to murder him ... but I couldn't do that so I tried to murder myself ... in a half-hearted sort of a way ... and they pumped my stomach and I got better and we tried to have another baby ... and found I was already pregnant ... and I thought she was Gavin's and Gavin thought she was Jim's ... so we both hated her ... and we did ... Jenny ... poor Jenny ... and I felt like dirt again and I ... well ... that's when I collapsed ... for years ... in and out of Gartnavel...

Oh no ... there's thousands like me ... nothing special about it ... nothing unusual...

And all the time, Morag looked at me like I was some kind of criminal, some kind of faithless, self-indulgent ... thief. Nobody was on my side... Nobody!

are not taking anything away from them that they ever really had.

I had told myself all those years that I would wait to leave till everyone was *ready*. So that it would all happen with the minimum of pain or fuss. But they weren't ready. Of course they weren't ready. No one is ever really ready. I wasn't ready for Daddy to die after those two years of pain. I wasn't ready to get married or ready when Clifford was born or ready for the depression after, or ready for Jennifer when she came along before I had recovered ... or for how guilty I felt when I failed her ... when I failed them all. When I failed to love them. I wasn't ready for Clifford being so lost after university or ready for his problems ... his depression ... his unemployment ... but I left them all anyway...

I was married to Gavin for thirty-two years. It was never supposed to happen. But Clifford was coming along and I quite liked Gavin and he was devoted ... to me ... so it seemed like the right thing ... everyone said how lucky I was and I believed them ... and like with the music, I did try to pretend ... for as long as I could ... but I had affairs ... I'm not ashamed of it ... I had affairs like my mother had had affairs ... and her mother ... oh yes ... Mummy told me ... years later ... right before the end ... when we sat up late and drank the sherry that probably killed her ... she told me lots of things I'm sure she never told Morag... But I made the mistake ... you see ... with this man ... out of all the men ... Jim Balfour ...

than making any kind of life for myself. My "self" didn't exist ... shouldn't exist. "I" was wrong. Oh, they kept asking me what "I" wanted ... but there was no "I" ... they'd seen to that. I can't even remember feeling like myself ... for year after year after year, that there was any such thing as me. The music I liked. The feelings I was supposed to have about my father and my husband and my sister and my children ... the causes and values I was supposed to believe in ... all that was theirs, never mine... It was corruption. And it worked. It worked. I was corrupted. They corrupted me. My feelings for Gavin, and for Jennifer and Clifford ... were alien ... things ... rituals ... and I felt like shit ... I really did. Like shit. Even the good feelings I was supposed to have ... felt forced on me and false, and I felt like some kind of monster for not feeling the way I was supposed to ... but I was a slave. I was. I was a slave. And a slave can love Massa's children ... but she knows it's a lie... So one day, the slave will stand in the burning house of her masters and look at the bloated, blackened corpses of the children she gave her life to loving and she will feel nothing. Blank eyed and terrible. That's who I was.

And all the things I walked away from when I finally left ... when I was finally free ... fell away from me so easily that I knew they had been nothing all along. I understood that I had never felt any of the things I was supposed to feel. And that freedom is pitiless. It has to be. Because it is total. It is hard. But you mustn't let them try and "guilt" you ... because you sex and sunshine ... cocaine and caviare ... would that be better? What would you prefer? What would make a better play? An adventuress who enjoys her adventures? Or a miserable saint exploding herself on a boulevard somewhere?

My father used to sit us ... Morag and me ... my father used to sit us both in the parlour ... yes ... we called it "the parlour" ... in the lovely house my mother's father's money had bought for us in Dowanhill... He sat us down in our parlour and warmed up his state-of-the-art stereogram and made us listen to things. One bloody concerto after another ... and on Sundays? God help us ... operas ... whole operas ... miserable kraut bitches warbling on about God knows what ... and Morag and Daddy sitting together studying the score while I looked at the libretto and wished I was dead ... and they would discuss the dramatic role of the woodwind and turn to me and ask me what I thought ... and what was I supposed to say? That child abuse comes in more than one disguise ... and when is some bloated tart going to sing me a song about THAT?

All my life ... all my life ... I allowed myself to be convinced by all of them, all of these "good" people at school and in my family ... that they knew what was best for me ... and that what was best for me was to sacrifice any chance of my happiness ... on the altar of their goodness. Their goodness. Not what was good for me. Just what was "good". So making a home for all of them was better and more important man... I am the mother of two grown-up children ... one of whom is doing very well and the other one bloody well isn't ... living with his useless father in a bedsit ... teaching himself how to play the guitar and writing a bloody novel ... as derelict at twenty-nine as his father is destroyed by his premature old age and preternatural tediousness at the age of sixty-two ... and what am I supposed to do now? Am I not supposed to live?

My father died when I was twenty ... my mother died last year ... she died, as it happens, while I was watching... I happened to be with her... I was looking after her when she had the stroke... Morag was away... Morag was out of the country ... and it was my decision ... what to do when they asked me the bloody question about the Liverpool Care Pathway ... oh, you know what that is, do you? ... and now ... thanks to mother ... I am a wealthy woman ... and I am absolutely delighted about it. There ... I've said it ... I've said the unsayable.

The solicitors have completed the sale ... today ... of mother's considerable assets... The whole portfolio of property and equity ... is now converted into ready cash. I am a free, wealthy, healthy woman. With no ties or obligations to anyone. What am I supposed to do now? What would you like me to do now...? Would you like me to sell all I have and give to the poor? I am not a character in a book. Would you? Would you really? Or would it be more interesting if I gave myself up entirely to indulgence ... sea, they think everyone else should be just as bloody miserable as they are. Bearded twits and stuffy matrons parading their neuroses as if it were supposed to be "depth", waving their issues in your face like somebody exposing themselves in a park ... multiculturalism and equality or some other self-regarding piffle, trying to drag those of us who just get on with life down to their level. As if there weren't enough to deal with what with the interest rates being at rock bottom and the terrorists blowing themselves up when one is on a perfectly innocent city break ... I mean, I've BEEN to those places ... Avenue Voltaire and the basilica at St Denis ... I've stayed in the Marais with all the Jewish people, and in the Ghetto Nuovo in Venice with armed bloody guards keeping the lunatics away. And ... yes ... I think that like it or not, we are all Israelis now... We are all hiding behind a bloody wall ... and thank God for it!

And don't tell me that all this mayhem is being caused by happy people, because it's not ... it's misfits and psychopaths making bombs and jihads out of their own personality problems ... who have fallen in love with their own misery and mistaken it for God ... and have made it their mission to make everyone else as miserable as they are... It is unhappy people who will quite happily blow you and themselves to smithereens because they don't like the way you pronounce the name of God.

I am a sixty-year-old woman ... the veteran of a long, dull marriage to a perfectly pleasant dull, dull that. Who does need that? I do not require the services of a playwright to make me a better person. I am in no need of improvement. I do not need to look at a picture I don't like until I "see something in it"... I will not sit through five hours of caterwauling at Scottish Opera for the sake of my soul. When I read, I do not want to be challenged, or to have my preconceptions turned inside out by the predicament of a middle-aged archaeology professor having a crisis with a female student and a small earthenware pot. I have no need of harrowing enlightenment. I have no use for a heart-stopping denouement. I like what I like, I am interested in what I am interested in and I don't want to be provoked, poked, upended or stimulated. I am not a crumbling Victorian property... I will not be improved. I am not an unweeded garden... I will not have you plant your flowers of culture in my topsoil. I do not see why my taxes and my admission money give anyone permission to shock and offend me. Nigella Lawson and Jamie Oliver between them provide me with all the challenges I need from literature, and I'll thank you and Melvyn Bragg to leave me alone in future.

I might take up yoga ... if that's any use to you... I quite fancy that... But I quite fancy going to India and doing it properly ... and not being bothered by the poverty one bit.

Allow me to tell you that I have personal experience of how much unhappy people are secretly enjoying themselves... They LIKE being like that ... that's why is the money ... Mummy's bloody money ... which is not the bloody theatre, and not the principles of quantum theory or the benefits or otherwise of cognitive therapy or what on earth I think I am doing leaving my bloody husband and what do I think is going to happen to my bloody children...?

No, Morag, we are not going to talk about any of that ... because that is not what we have got to talk about. You do not get to lecture me about being a good daughter or a good wife or a good pupil. We are not ten years old and I am not going to have anyone rub out the word "choc-o-late" with my face...

My face. Our face... Well not for much longer... When the surgeons are done with me, my mouth will be reshaped, my nose will be reduced and my cheekbones will finally have the definition they deserve and nobody will mistake me for you... I have met a wonderful man, I am properly happy for the first time I can remember, and I will not take lectures from you or anyone about what I am doing wrong with my life and how I shouldn't forget about the rainforest, the mountain leopards, the refugees and global bloody warming!

I expect this play is going to try to teach me something too... I bet it will try to make me think! Really ... it's so insulting ... as if we need some self-righteous public school boy's instructions on how to think! As if we need some lesbian with a guilt complex exposing herself in order to stimulate an intellectual or moral response. I don't need that. You don't need

It's funny what families are like ... because buggering off away from this bloody cold, serious, guilt inducing country is exactly what Mummy would have done herself ... a generation later ... if she could have ... if she'd ever had the chance ... and it's exactly what I've done NOW, I suppose, later in life ... now that I've left Gavin to stew in his own juices ... with Morag and the lamented ghost of my dear dead father looking down on me ... disapproving of me. Worrying about me.

Worrying about me? It's a joke. A stupid, Scottish joke.

I have a positive attitude. I always have had. And guess what? Now I'm a grown-up? Now that I'm myself? People like me. I am a success. I have friends. All over the world. People respond to my energy.

Look at you. You're responding.

I had thought I was coming here to meet my sister. I booked the tickets for that purpose, not that I could make head or tail of the website... And not that she's turned up. Where has she got to?

(she looks around)

It was of course her idea that we come here in order to be "normal" ... to talk about the play ... talk about what's on the news ... and not the real and only subject we really have to talk about, Morag ... which

Of people telling me what was right or wrong. And I was never not in trouble. I've never not been in trouble of one sort or another to this very day ... ever since... No ... of course I never told my parents... You didn't. In Scotland? In the 1960s? Don't be ridiculous! Teachers and doctors and lawyers ... policemen and politicians ... ministers ... were all quite beyond questioning... By anyone, let alone by children... Even though my father was paying fees to these psychopaths for the privilege of my being brutalised like that.

After, I did all sorts of things ... smoking ... shoplifting ... and boys, of course ... as soon as they were interested of course ... and interesting...

My father and Morag ... I remember the two of them, all through my childhood ... being so CONCERNED ... about what I'd COME to ... what I was MAKING of myself ... and yes ... they were both teachers. My father was a teacher ... till his illness ... and Morag is still a teacher... Both of them...

Not that we lived like teachers. Oh no. Mother had money, you see... Her father was the owner of a very successful "chain" ... I suppose you'd call it now ... of shoe shops. George Larbert and son. Grandpa was the son. Not that I ever knew him. He died when I was very young ... and granny sold the shops and buggered off to the Riviera on the proceeds ... leaving Mum and Uncle Ronnie...

in my head ... damn her ... I suppose that's what education means ... bastards like that ... still in your head ... half a century later...

Even then Morag was a favourite ... with teachers ... grown-ups in general ... because she was so clever and precocious and interested in music and art and all the things that proper young ladies ... and Mrs MacKay ... her face softened ... I can still see it ... into a simper like the Grinch in that old Christmas cartoon ... and she said ... "Isobel?" ... and I had the sentence... She gave it to me ... deliberately...

"Andrew's father very nicely gave us all a treat of lemonade and..." I said it... I said it like any normal Scottish person ... and normal British person from the twentieth bloody century would say it... I heard myself saying the worst thing that anyone on earth could ever say ... "choclit" ... and she stood me up ... and she called me out in front of the class ... and she wrote the word on the board ... CHOC-O-LATE "Do you see that?" she said. "Do you see that, you wicked girl?" and she rubbed it out with my face... She held my hair and she rubbed it out with my face ... so I'd never forget. She held my hair ... and rubbed the word out ... with my face ... and I sat down ... all chalk and tears and snotters ... and Morag whispered to me ... "sorry" ... and do you know ... I've never forgotten. So I suppose they'd call that a success.

I was never a great fan ... of education after that.

that to say "chocklit" was a lazy Americanism and an insult to Shakespeare or something ... not that I ever remember her explaining that ... in fact I only really remember one thing ... and that was the time the wicked old bitch set us a reading passage ... with that bloody word in it ... choc-o-late...

Of course now I think about it as an adult I bet she did it deliberately, that she was sitting there righteous and prim in her purple permanent and flesh-coloured maxi suit WAITING for that word to come around. Because we'd all seen it ... of course we had... There it was ... two-thirds of the way down the page ... and we were all reading a sentence each ... and I remember ... vividly, counting the heads in the desks in front and beside me and sighing with relief as I saw that bloody word wouldn't come anywhere near me...

Everyone was counting ... as if it were a lesson in arithmetic as well as received English pronunciation ... and she must have known we were counting, the old cow ... because she suddenly skipped a row and I couldn't tell any more if it would be me... I started sweating ... can you imagine...? I was ten years old in a sweat of physical fear... I felt sick ... and I could see ... that it would be either Morag ... or me... We sat together in her class ... what was her bloody name? ... and the sentence was coming ... and it was going to be Morag's turn ... but even then ... even then Morag was...

Mrs MacKay ... that was her name ...! She's still

it isn't virtuous or self-sacrificing ... not a bit of it. Giving works. And Morag and I are the living proof. We're an experiment. Socially, personally, financially – in every way, identical twins, both girls, both brought up in the same family under the same circumstances at exactly the same time ... same education ... and different outcomes ... utterly, utterly different ... and why? Because we've been different from birth ... genetics be bothered! Everyone at school could see it ... pupils, teachers ... everyone...

Yet I was always ... I was always the one ... who was supposed to feel guilty ... who was always wrong ... who was supposed to be punished...

Not that I'm bitter about it any more. It's all a long time ago.

There was one teacher at our school ... mad as a hatter now I think of it ... we were only ten years old. For instance ... she would tie a knot in her handkerchief and wet it in the sink in the classroom before beating you with it ... over the head ... saving the belt for special occasions. And girls would literally wet themselves rather than raise their hands and say they wanted to go to the bathroom. Oh, quite potty ... purple hair, INCHES of face powder ... we thought she looked like the surface of the moon ... all cracks and craters ... and she had this obsession ... obsession! ... with correcting the English language... Choc-o-late ... she would insist that the word choc-o-late be pronounced exactly as it was spelled... She maintained

(laughs)

That is absolutely one of my favourite words... It sounds exactly like the thing it is ... as if the lady in question were letting go of the most enormous fart underneath her layers of skirt and cardigan ... yes ... so at least there's time to walk away!

She doesn't really try, poor thing ... but it isn't just external appearance ... it's an inner radiance ... it's happiness, really, isn't it? Not happy, not lucky. Not our Morag... And with my face ... in a way it's my face ... but it's your attitude ... your attitude to life ... the way that you set about the task of living it ... day by day ... that's what counts. The glass is half-full or half-empty, isn't it? It's your attitude ... your attitude is your essence. Will you excuse me...

(she writes)

No, it's just funny how one thought can lead you to another, if you let it... So what I was just thinking is that no matter what the scientists say ... we are not just the sum of our genetics ... are we? Our experiences and our attitudes change who we are because the kind of experiences we have come from our attitudes and vice versa...

(she writes)

... I have a positive attitude. I give. I try to. I do. And I don't want to sound immodest or virtuous because

Yes. I always carry a notebook. It's a tool of the trade. I did think you might have recognised me, you were looking at me in a peculiar way ... but I thought it was because you had mistaken me for my sister, Morag... She comes to these sort of events when she can. We're identical twins, you see...

Oh, we're very different people. I think that's the charitable way of putting it. No one who knows either of us at all well could ever mistake us one for the other.

Morag ... poor Morag... She's not exactly a ray of sunshine if you follow... Morag has never been one to walk into a room and fill it with her personality... She's more of a drain than a generator ... energetically considered. Not her fault. Poor thing. Oh yes ... she's a terrific culture vulture. This is just her kind of place...

Still ... we have the same face ... for the moment.

Mind you, it's a much more regular occurrence for poor old Morag to get mistaken for me ... and then everyone ends up disappointed...

Though funnily enough, even when we were at school and wore the same uniform, we weren't often mistaken for each other. And our parents were very insistent we not dress alike outside of school ... even if we'd wanted to. And anyway ... God love her, you'd see if she was here, God forgive me ... but Morag is a bit of a frump.

ACT 1

A well-dressed woman of sixty takes her seat in a lunch-time theatre. She busies herself with a notebook, waiting for the performance to start. Eventually, she turns to another audience member.

ISOBEL

Do you come to a lot of these? It's supposed to be very popular. This is my first. Well, normally, I simply wouldn't have the time.

When does it start? Should it not have have started already? They've obviously got time on their hands … on both sides of the footlights.

Personally, I've never liked the theatre very much. Even worse when it's all serious about some "issue" or other. Trying to make you feel guilty. I suppose some people like it. Possibly because it reminds them of church. Actually, if you'll excuse me, that's quite good. I'll just write that down.

(she gets out her notebook and begins to write)

... there's an implied unflattering portrait of Scotland in this terrific new double monologue by Peter Arnott; a place where a need for respectability runs deep, but real love for humanity is in short supply, and easily swept away by the temptations of wealth and sex.

... Isobel is far less dislikeable than she sounds; partly because the kind of over-respectable background she comes from is all too recognisable, and ripe for rebellion, and partly because of the decades of profound pain it caused her, which her new can-do attitude can barely disguise.

... Yet this solo play is also an unforgettable portrait of an individual woman; far too fiercely intelligent to deny her status as an elderly, unloved figure, but bold enough to feel that that status does not define her worth, and that in the end - even with the face her sister has rejected - being Morag is really quite all right, ...

Joyce McMillan, *The Scotsman*, 10 and 17 February 2016

Face – Isobel and Morag

Happily for the publisher, these plays are almost as good on the page as they were on the stage, and that difference is due to the virtuoso performance of Janette Foggo who impersonated these irreconcilable souls with verve and intelligence.

    Allan Cameron, Glasgow, 30 March 2016

shine through the heavy layers of self-deception. And courage of a kind – perhaps the best kind.

Isobel wishes to subvert everything and in particular the *bien pensant* of the Glasgow middle classes. Initially it feels as though this is quite a simple woman, "shallow" as the father is supposed to have said. But her insistence on her own amorality becomes less credible during the play, just as her happiness proves more explicitly to have no historical basis. She is obsessed with or challenged by morality, whether sham or not, and this surely demonstrates that morality is not as insignificant to her as she claims. She is something of an unreliable narrator, and a very funny one at that.

When we meet Morag, we feel that we already know her because we have heard what her sister has had to say about her. Unsurprisingly her accounts of shared events are very different from her sister's, and neither are particularly credible. The audience reinterprets them continuously, but most likely each of them does so in a different manner. The inability to know and to understand is one of the many themes of the play. Though probably even more misanthropic than her sister, Morag is more honest, particularly when it comes to herself or at least her awareness of how other people see her. Her intellectual superiority is as gruesome as Isobel's live-life-to-the-full ambitions. Their desires destroy them, but Arnott is the great writer he is because through all this – and we laugh at them throughout the play – he gifts them with a humanity that reminds that we're not so different ourselves.

Introduction

Peter Arnott's plays, *Face – Isobel* and *Face – Morag*, were performed at Oran Mòr, Glasgow in February 2016 on consecutive weeks, but they can be looked on as a single work. It takes great skill to extract so much from the simple idea of monologues by two contrasting identical twins: that's two minds who share the same face and the same family, culture, class, nation and perhaps most importantly generation. It is the multiplicity of often conflicting ideas that makes it so difficult to summarise this work.

Isobel starts on a high note of optimism and bravado, and this reminds me of something I have always believed: happy people don't boast about being happy, unhappy people do. Happy people don't even know they're happy until they're unhappy. Happiness usually can involve any form of absorption that isn't self-absorption, and these two are very self-absorbed. As the play develops, it becomes clear that Isobel is far from happy, though she puts a heroically brave face on it all, as will her sister. Perhaps we're all a bit of Isobel and a bit of Morag, or along a spectrum between them. In other words deeply flawed, but also sharing momentary glimmers of self-awareness that

© Peter Arnott 2016

First published in April 2016 by
Vagabond Voices Publishing Ltd.,
Glasgow,
Scotland.

ISBN 978-1-908251-66-4

The author's right to be identified as author of this book under the Copyright, Designs and Patents Act 1988 has been asserted.

Printed and bound in Poland

Cover design by Mark Mechan

Typeset by Park Productions

The publisher acknowledges subsidy towards this publication from Creative Scotland

ALBA | CHRUTHACHAIL

For further information on Vagabond Voices, see the website, www.vagabondvoices.co.uk

Face – Isobel and Morag

Two monologues

by

Peter Arnott

Vagabond Voices
Glasgow